YOGA & NATUROPATHY

...FOR DIABETES

YOGA & NATUROPATHY

...FOR DIABETES

By

Acharya Krishna Deo

Worldwide Published by

Pendown Press

PENDOWN PRESS
An ISO 9001 & ISO 14001 certified Co.,
Regd. Office: 2525/193, 1st Floor, Onkar Nagar-A,
Tri Nagar, Delhi-110035
Ph.: 09350849407, 09312235086
Branch Office: 1A/2A, 20, Hari Sadan, Ansari Road,
Daryaganj, New Delhi-110002
Ph.: 011-45794768
Website: PendownPress.com

First Edition: 2018
Price: ₹279/
ISBN: 978-93-88149-53-2

Layout and Cover Designed by Pendown Graphics Team
Printed and Bound in India by Thomson Press India Ltd.

BIOGRAPHY

An Introduction to Acharya Krishna Deo

Acharya Krishna Deo is a humanitarian, spiritual teacher, poet and an ambassador of peace and compassion. His vision of healthy, happy and peaceful society has united people from all walks of life, over through service projects and the programs/ courses of World Welfare Mission *'Aanandmay Jeevan- The Art of Blissful Life!'* Social *Shivir* and Corporate Workshop.

The Beginning

- Born in 1976 in India. *Acharya Ji* was often found practicing yoga, meditation and worship since his childhood. He could very well recite the verses of *Bhagwad Geeta* and other Holy Scriptures during primary school days!

His Holiness *Swami Vivekananda* is his inspirational *Guru! Sri Ramakrishna Paramhansa's* preaching from *Upanishad:*

// आत्मनो मोक्षार्थम् जगत्हिताय च //

'Aatmano mokshartham jagadhitaya cha!'

"Our life is for the sake of our self-liberation as well as for the good of the world"! This divine massage *became* the ultimate purpose of his life!

And at the same time his interest was into modern science specially Life Sciences, during his academic days.

His longing to search the science of divinity and to experience infinite energy, he began his journey in 1995 and visited almost all big and small religious Ashrams and holy places to help millions of people around the world, for their physical, emotional and social problems. He attended *Satsangs* for years to experience divine love and art of blissful life!

In his journey to such divine places, he received the blessings in form of divine wisdom, self-awareness, soul upliftment and enlightment from Rarefied Saints - Himalayan Ascetic, Enlightened Gurus, Yogis, Sages and Spiritual masters! He also visited modern medical science and naturopathy institutions for years to research the modern and ancient nature healing — drugless techniques.

Acharya ji is lifetime member and advisor of some world-class Spiritual and Health organizations. Remaining a beginner at all times!?

Foundation of the 'World Welfare Mission'

After serving many years as a Yoga faculty, social activist and wellness Guru, *Acharya Krishna Deo* established *World Welfare Mission* in 2005, to spread Health, Happiness, Peace and Welfare around the world; A non-profit organization with a mission to work towards the betterment of the individuals, the society and the world. The organization undertakes several social, environmental and holistic wellness programs with the help of its volunteers. Wide range of social, environmental, cultural and spiritual activities reaches all walks of life with the onerous and dedicated effort of the World Welfare Mission. A volunteer based non-political, educational, humanitarian organization; it is committed to creating peace by uplifting the levels of the individuals and fostering human values within the global community. It is based out of New Delhi and has a presence in several countries.

Inspiring Selfless Service and Globalizing 'The Art of Blissful Life!'

A noted humanitarian leader, *Acharya Krishna Deo's* programs have provided assistance to people from a wide range of people of all age groups and communities. The strength of his message has inspired a wave of service based on spirituality through groups of dedicated volunteers, who are driving these projects forward in critical areas around the globe.

As a spiritual healer, *Acharya ji* has rekindled the traditions of yoga, meditation, cosmic energy, nature cure and offered them in a form that is relevant to the current century. Beyond reviving ancient wisdom, *Acharya ji* has created new techniques for personal and social transformations.

Through his initiatives and addresses, *Acharya ji* has consistently emphasized the need for reinforcing human values and recognizing humanity as our highest identity. Fostering interfaith harmony and calling for multi-cultural education as the remedy for fanaticism are significant parts of his efforts to achieve sustainable peace and love on our planet.

His work has touched the lives of people around the world, going beyond the barriers of race, nationality and religion with the message of a "One Global Family"; that inner and outer peace are possible; and that a stress-free, ailment free and violence-free society can be created through selfless service and the reawakening of human values and self-awareness.

Conducting Social, Corporate workshop and seminars on:

'Aanandmay Jeevan–The Art of Blissful life!'

Program Topics:

1. Corporate Yoga
2. Chair Yoga
3. Desktop Yoga
4. Food Therapy— Nature Care Diet Plan
5. Power Yoga
6. Mantra Yoga
7. *Yogasana* (Needful Yogic Postures)
8. *Pranayama* (More than 26 Yogic Breathing Science and Process)
9. Healing Meditation Process (More than 112 Meditation techniques)
10. *Vipassana* Meditation

11. *Kundalini Dhyan*/Chakra Meditation

12. Karmic Cleansing Meditation

13. Yogic Game/Play activities

14. Music Meditation/Therapy

- Therapeutic Yoga and Food Therapy. Yoga and Nature Cure for Precaution and Cure. Cure in illness, Care in wellness!

Therapeutic Yoga and Food Therapy training to handle Lifestyle disorders, like:

Stress, Depression, Anger, B.P. (low/high), Thyroid, Back pain, Arthritis, Diabetes, Hypertension, Gastro, Constipation, Asthma, Obesity, Cervical, Joint pain, Sinus , Infertility, Obesity, Acidity, Drowsiness, Concentration, IQ level and almost every related problems.

- Quantum Healing—The science of cosmic energy!
- Distance Healing
- Spiritual counseling
- Obesity Management
- Insomnia Management (Sleep Disorders Mgmt)
- Yogic Relaxation Process
- Yogic Diet and Lifestyle
- Everyday Health & Wellness awareness program
- Yogic Relaxation Process (IRT and QRT)
- Laughter Yoga Workshop
- Anti Ageing Workshop
- Dancing Meditation Workshop

- Stress Management Workshop
- Anger Management Workshop

Other Needful Programs

- Leadership & Motivational Training Program
- Art of Divine Parenting Workshop!
- Food Therapy- Nature Care Diet plan!
- Personal & Professional life balance
- Positive Attitude & Lifestyle Workshop
- Cosmic Energy/Law of attraction for mental programming
- One to one Personal counseling (Health, Stress and Depression)
- Techniques (*Kriya*) of self-awareness/awakening and more...

Transformative Management Programs

- Life Management Techniques Based on *Bhagwad Gita*
- Management Principles from *Bhagwad Geeta*
- Corporate Success with *Bhagwad Gita*
- Personal Excellence and Management Excellence Through *Bhagawad Gita*)

A Spiritual Motivation talk and activity based program for corporate and social groups, based on timeless wisdom from authentic scriptures and teachings of great spiritual masters.

- **For Holistic Wellness:** Health-Happiness-Peace-Divine Love and Harmony.

- We see this beautiful world as A Divine Global Family spreading blissful life management and CSR- Corporate Spiritual Responsibility!
- Yoga Methods: *Ashtanga Yoga, Bhakti Yoga, Raj Yoga, Karma Yoga, Gyan Yoga, Kundalini Yoga, Mantra Yoga, Seva Yoga* and more.....

"*Aanandmay Jeevan-* The Art of Blissful Life" programme have been organized and appreciated by prominent organisations like:

- Bank of India
- Delhi police
- Encore Capital group
- Genpact (AIG)
- HSIL (Hindustan Sanitary ware & Industries Ltd)
- HHI (Hotel Hindusthan International-5 star)
- ITBP (The Indo- Tibetan Border Police)
- Indian Army
- ISKCON
- L & T
- Lions Club International
- MRV School Dwarka
- Ojas Tennis Academy
- Rotary Club (The Park Hotel-5 Star)
- Shalimar Paints Ltd
- Samsung Electronics
- Syndicate Bank

- Schneider Electric, DLF Cyber City, Gurgaon
- Sangh Sree-Nagrik Swasthya Sangha
- SMITHY group (ARCVAC)
- The Air Force of India
- News 24 (TV News Channel)
- ZEE TV
- And many more ......

To know more about our mission kindly visit: www.worldwelfaremission.org

HUMBLE GRATITUDE!

I owe my humble gratitude to my beloved parents, for my proper grooming to their sincere desire and liking so that they can find me as a good human being. I bow to your feet for all your unconditional love, care and blessings! *Matri devo bhav, Pitri devo bhav!*

- To *"Avadhashram Pariwar"* all beloved members with very high Reverence!
- To all my *Gurus* (Great Masters) of Academic life and Spiritual life! *Acharya devo bhav!*
- Unfathomable source of wisdom: The Vedas, *Upnishads*, *Vedanta, Geeta, Ramayana* and all the holy books and Yoga scriptures that I read!.
- *Sri Dhiraj jee, Chetna* and *Mridul - Manav* for all your love and support. It would not have been possible without you to begin my spiritual journey, flawlessly!
- Many more personalities whose names are worth mentionable, I remember them and remain grateful for sharing my efforts in fulfilling my dreams to help the society!
- I am thankful to these organizations, their masters and the teachings which inspired me a lot:
- Ram Krishna Math/Mission-Belur Math (Swami Vivekananda).
- *Yogoda Satsanga* Society of India (*Sri Sri Paramahansa Yogananda*).
- The Art of Living Foundation.

- Transcendental Meditation (*Maharishi Mahesh Yogi*).
- Laughter Yoga Club International.
- *Patanjali Yogpeeth – Haridwar.*
- Bihar School of Yoga – *Munger Math (Swami Shivananda Saraswati).*
- *Shanti Kunja/Gayatri Pariwar- Haridwar (Sri Ram Sharma Acharya).*
- Brahma Kumaries Ishwariya Vishwa Vidyalaya.
- ISKCON – International Society for Krishna Consciousness (*Srila Prabhupada*)
- Global *Vipassana* Foundation (*Sri S.N. Goenka*).
- I am thankful to Almighty God! Thank you for sending me on this beautiful planet to serve. I feel fortunate that you are keeping me engaged in the holy service of your devotees. It is all your pure love and grace!! You are always with me!!!

"त्वमेव माता च पिता त्वमेव
त्वमेव बंधू च सखा त्वमेव!
त्वमेव विद्‍या, द्रविणं त्वमेव,
त्वमेव सर्वं मम देव देव!!"

"O! Supreme Lord, only you are my mother, father, relative and friend. You are only my knowledge and wealth. You are my everything.

ABOUT THE AUTHOR

Acharya Krishna Deo is a renowned spiritual master, poet, writer and an ambassador of peace & harmony. His vision of healthy, happy and peaceful society has united people from all walks of life. He has made his presence felt through the service projects and the programs/courses of World Welfare Mission '*Aanandmay Jeevan*—The Art of Blissful Life!'.

The Life Journey of Acharya Ji

- Born in 1976 in India, *Acharya Krishna Deo* started his spiritual journey in 1995 and in a quest to search the science of divinity and experience infinite energy first hand, he visited almost all big and small religious Ashrams and holy places.
- *Acharya Ji* established *World Welfare Mission* in 2005, to spread Health, Happiness, Peace & Welfare around the world.

ABOUT THE BOOK

The present book covers all the essentials of traditional as well as the modern-day yoga. The chapter *Pranayama* has 4 yogic breathing process while the chapter on healing meditation process contains 5 meditation techniques.

The chapters are interlinked in such a way so that the book itself becomes a compendium of knowledge for its readers—explaining every query, answering all the questions, opening every aspect of yoga, and underlining its every aspect.

The book contains almost all the contemporary topics of Yoga along with its modern offshoots, such as Nature cure Food Therapy to handle lifestyle-related disorders, such as Stress, Depression, Anger, B.P (low/high), Thyroid, Back pain, Arthritis, Diabetes, Hypertension, Gastro, Constipation, Asthma, Obesity, Cervical, Joint pain, Sinus, Infertility, Obesity, Acidity, Drowsiness, Lack of Concentration, IQ level etc. This book will certainly help its readers attain good health and enlightenment through the practice of Yoga and meditation.

CONTENTS

Biography....................v

Humble Gratitude!....................xiii

About the Author....................xv

About the Book....................xvii

Chapter-1

Yoga for Blissful Life!....................1-16

Chapter-2

Yogasana....................17-54

I. Prayer with Om Chanting

II. Toning up of the Body

III. Self Love

IV. Butterfly Pose

V. Tadasana

VI. Kapalbhati Kriya

VII. Bhastrika Pranayama

VIII. Naukasana (Boat Pose)

IX. Dhanurasana

X. Mandukasana (Frog Pose)

XI. Agnisar Pranayama

XII. Nadi Shodhan Pranayama (Alternate Nostril Breathing Technique)

XIII. Surya Namaskara

XIV. Paschimottanasana

XV. Pawan Muktasana

XVI. Uttanapadasana

Chapter-3

Nature Cure..55-63

I. Kunjal

II. Naturopathy

III. Hip Bath

IV. Cold Hip Bath

V. Hot Hip Bath

VI. Neutral Hip Bath

VII. Alternate Hip Bath

VIII. Mud Therapy

Chapter-4

Diet Plan..65-67

Chapter-5

Meditation..69-78

I. Witness your breath (*Shwas Preksha* or *Anapan Sati*)

II. Witness your stomach (*Udar Preksha*)

III. Vipassana Meditation

IV. Body Scan Meditation

V. Yog Nidra in Shavasana

Chapter-6

Tips on Sleep Disorders (Insomnia)........................79-84

Chapter-7

About 'World Welfare Mission'..................................85-91

Chapter-8

Project Ashram...93-97

YOGA FOR BLISSFUL LIFE!

Why Yoga?

Medical studies conducted worldwide have now proved that the practice of yoga can reduce the level of stress to its practitioner from the very first class itself. A diligent daily practice of yoga will help you return to your work refreshed and rejuvenated, not only physically, but mentally as well.

Science behind Yoga

Yoga as a Complete Science Refers to:

1. The structural anatomy of the body
2. The physiology of the body, organs and glands
3. The bond between glands and hormones
4. The relationship between energy pulses (frequency or vibration) and sound

5. The brain, its perceptions, thought patterns and brain chemistry
6. Thought as a vibration and how it affects
7. Consciousness as the observer

Then Yoga is performed

- As light exercises and Yogic postures to align the physical components of the body and stimulate rejuvenation of cells in all organs and glands
- **As relaxation techniques**: for balancing the flow of energy and releasing.
- *Pranayama*: particular way of breathing to charge and empower body and mind
- **Meditation and concentration**: to engage in some sorts of mental exercises for adjusting brain chemistry in order to bring clarity of perception, tranquility as well as emotional stability.

How does the practice of Yoga Heal the Body?

- The movements of the body parts in a certain way enhances both the circulation of blood and lymphatic fluids which enable the body tissues to release toxins and receive fresh nutrients.
- Several deep-breathing exercises make the blood enriched with oxygen. Oxygen is regarded as the number one element for the body as it is a must for our very survival and its deficit lowers our immunity and low immunity power results into a variety of diseases.

- Relaxation techniques are used to bring down the stress levels in muscles, the nervous system as well as the mind.
- The stretches in Yoga release the tension from the muscles and joints. The stretches in Yoga helps release the tension from various joints and muscles.
- The practice of yoga develops mental clarity and focus thereby enhancing concentration and augmenting the healing process.
- Spiritual awakening brings realization of our eternal nature and subsequent peace of mind. Spiritual awakening paves the way for the realization of our eternal nature and ultimately peace of mind.
- practising
- The practitioners of yoga themselves notice the improvements in their energy level, fitness, reliefs and prevention in their stress-related problems and enhancement in their immune systems. Business persons have found it as a cost-effective, morale booster and employee retention aide.

Who can Perform Yoga?

Anyone can perform yoga, regardless of their age or physical condition; however, the yoga that they perform may vary because of the varying individual needs.

For example, athletes and dancers can practice for restoring the energy and to improve stamina; house wives for rejuvenating the energy and to reduce fatigue; executives to give a break to the overworked mind;

children to control the wandering mind, muscle toning, to improve memory and concentration; seniors to feel strong, and to improve memory.

Breathing techniques (popularly known as *pranayama*) is regarded as one of the most powerful tools as it works as a tonic to reduce headache, the level of stress, insomnia, emotional imbalance, etc. In fact, a child of 5 years to a person of ripe old age can perform yoga.

While starting a yoga practice without the support of a qualified yoga teacher is not recommended, we acknowledge that many people do not have access to a teacher due to location or times of classes.

We have put all our available resources here to help you start a yoga practice.

Goals: While it is good to have goals for your yoga practice (building strength, reducing stress, obtaining flexibility, losing weight), it is not good to be focused only on obtaining them. Yoga is a process, and sometimes this process can be very slow (so have patience). Use your goals to help select the type and level of postures you wish to practice.

When not to do yoga

Before doing yoga, it is important to read the contraindications for each posture. There are certain medical conditions/symptoms, such as menstruation, pregnancy, high blood pressure and injuries to the knees shoulders and neck where doing certain postures is prevented. Special care needs to be taken in almost all postures.

If you have any medical condition, you should check with your health care professional before starting a yoga practice.

Variations and modifications

The instructions and pictures of the yoga postures are the goal as to where you are going towards, not trying to be. Keep on doing experiments and explore several positions as well as alignment in order to make the posture work for your body.

Place

If possible, one should practice Yoga in open space. However, that place should be pollution free. However, in today's polluted atmosphere of urban cities, it is better to practice in a spacious and tidy room.

Equipments

Take a yoga mat or any mat that acts as anti-conductor of earthing.

You can practice on chair/sofa or bed also. Meditation and *pranayama* you practice in temple/*Pooja ghar* for better concentration. There are no specific equipments required as such for Yoga practices. However, you can use round pillow, candle, sitting pillow, music, fragrance, etc. for meditation, *pranayama* and *Tratak.*

Music: Soothing music along with better surroundings invariably make your mind feel relaxed and stable within.

It may be *Bhajan* (devotional/spiritual music/song/ Prayer), natural sounds of wind, birds, fountain, waterfall, bay of ocean. Indian classical music, instrumental like flute, harmonium, guitar, *santoor* etc.

Fragrance

Fragrances are as good as soothing music.

Create better surroundings with good fragrance of your choice, flowers, sandalwood, incense stick; aromatic candles etc. would be good for your mind, body and soul.

Duration

Depending on your work engagement, you can stretch your practice between 15 to 90 minutes and 3-6 times per week.

This depends on what is desired from Yoga. If the need is basic flexibility of the body and stress-relief, one can be benefited in just twenty minutes. To relieve particular diseases, one can practice in morning and evening both but at least two hours before going to bed, empty stomach. If one wants spiritual enlightment, four to five hours are also not enough. As far as the time duration for maintaining a posture is concerned, you can start with ten seconds and extend this up to thirty seconds in a minute.

This depends on what is desired from Yoga. If the need is basic flexibility of the body and stress-relief, one can be benefited in just twenty minutes. To relieve particular diseases, one can practice in morning and evening both but at least two hours before going to bed, empty stomach. If one wants spiritual enlightment, four to five hours are also not enough. As far as the time duration for maintaining a posture is concerned, you can start with ten seconds and extend this up to thirty seconds in a minute.

Posture selection

You need not choose a practice posture that causes inconvenience to you. Postures done on the floor are going to be easier that standing postures as they do not require as much strength or balance. In addition, postures that have longer recommended hold times (in breaths) are going to be easier to do.

Repetition

At the beginning, you should practice each *asana* one time, and try to maintain each posture for as long as you can. Gradually, you can repeat each asana for 2 to 10 times as per your strength and goal.

Breathing

Your breathings must be normal and devoid of any sorts of inconveniences during postures. When you bend forward, exhale, while coming upward or bending backward, inhale. This is a simple rule.

What to wear: Though you may wear comfortable or tight clothes, but if you wear flexible dress, it will work better.

It's important to wear something that will not restrict your movement. These could vary from being skin-tight to very loose as per your convenience.

Drinking/eating

Empty stomach is a must for performing yoga. Hence, the ideal timing is within two hours of sun rise or after two hours of sunset. Mind, when you perform yoga in the evening, the ideal time will be 5 hours after lunch.

It is not advisable to eat or drink right before a yoga practice (especially if you are practising inversions). Eat 1-3 hours before and drink only small amounts of water before practice, and do not drink during your practice (only small amount can be taken if needed). After 15 to 30 minutes of practices, you can eat.

Bath

One can perform Yoga after bath or go for bath after 20-30 minutes of finishing the Yoga practices when body is in normal temperature and relaxed.

Regularity

Mind, Yoga is not only a therapy, but also a way of life.

So it is as essential as food and water for life, it should be practiced every day. However, three days, four days, five days and six days per week according to your convenience is good, but continuity always plays a greater role.

Combination of *Asanas*

If you perform a forward-bending posture, do a backward-bending posture after that. For a complete Yoga workout, you should select postures for every part of the body.

These include standing, sitting and lying postures (lying on the back-supine line, lying on the stomach- prone line).

Order of Yoga practices: There is no any rule for that. Different Yoga gurus teach different yogic orders. So, never be confused in orders. Practice in your comfortable choice of orders.

How to start

It will be better if you begin your practice with a brief meditation. Come into easy pose close your eyes and breathe deeply. You can alternately practice a *Pranayama* as you meditate.

How to end

It is advisable to conclude your practice with *Savasana/ Yogindrasana*, relaxation posture.

This allows the body to integrate all of the postures and to balance and absorb the *prana*/energy, which has been created and released during your practice. This is also one of the most important practices for stress management.

Daily Regimen

Several hours of long processes of practice will be needed, if you are willing to become a master yogi, capable of getting all the beneficial effects of yoga.

However, making a start is the crucial step. Beginners can follow a basic daily yoga program to start on the path towards good health. This is a simplified program to rejuvenate your health through yoga practices each day and a step-by-step guide to executing common therapeutic postures.

Basic Precautions of Yoga

Yoga imposes certain disciplines for a balanced and contented life.

These disciplines are not erroneous. Rather, all these have scientific justifications.

Unlike superficial, frivolous lifestyles without any do's or don'ts, the regular practice of yoga helps by cultivating character, good eating, cleansing, proper breathing and relaxation. It is designed to awaken the characteristics of what it means in life to be human.

One should remember that:

1. Practising yoga in the wrong manner make increase the negativities, rather than developing positive changes in the body and mind.

   When practising asana it is important to use common sense and to watch the reactions of your body, thereby judging the time that you stay in them.

   Therefore, it is advisable to seek the guidance of an experienced teacher and to tick to his or her suggestions

   According to one's ability, suppleness of body and constitution. You should not perform yoga without suitable professional guidance and knowledge.

2. Weak patients are warned against holding their breath (*Kumbhaka*) during *pranayama*.

3. If you are among those persons, who are suffering from some serious health complications, such as heart trouble, high or low blood pressure, or any serious organic diseases, you should not try to hold your breath during *Pranayama*.
4. Practice in the presence of a medical or yoga expert.
5. Sweating during practice: Instead of wiping the body with a towel, rub the body with palms.
6. After performing *Pranayama* and *asanas*, avoid doing some strenuous physical exercises, such as weightlifting, gymnastics, jogging, tennis, swimming, etc. Allow at least 20 to 30 minutes after yoga before other exercises.

   The sequence of yogic practices; *Kriyas, Asanas, Pranayama, Chittashuddhi* and Yoga *Nidra/Shavasana* should be maintained.
7. In attaining peace of mind, yoga should be practiced in a quiet, secluded place, where fresh air envelops you for fresh breathing of the mind.
8. Women having menstrual period (before and after 2-3 days) and pregnancy should avoid doing any abdominal asana. However, there is no any restriction on performing *Pranayama* and meditations.

   Gradually start *yogasana* after three months of delivery.
9. Person having any surgery in last two years, Appendicitis, Ulcer, Hernia etc. should not practice any abdominal practices.

10. Medical Problems: People with specific problems that need immediate medical intervention, should consult their doctor prior to performing any Yoga.
11. It is recommended that you either practice early in the morning, or in early evening on a relatively empty stomach.
12. You are allowed to practice yoga four hours after a heavy meal and 30 minutes after a glass of juice or a cup of skimmed milk.
13. Avoid fried food and spices, tea, coffee, smoking, alcohol, *zarda*, pan *masala*, sweets, etc.

    As they activate chemical toxins, which are harmful and cause stress and illness.
14. Raw food, salad and fruits should comprise your daily diet.

    Drink at least 8-10 glasses of water every day, irrespective of yogic practice. It helps in cleaning up the system.
15. Make a time schedule for performing the yoga practice and make it a regular habit.

    For instance, *Pranayama* can be started with a less duration initially and can be later increased gradually depending on one's capability to concentrate.
16. In the beginning, you may feel stiffness in muscles. But, if you are regular in your practice, the stiffness will ease.

    Physical comfort is as important as mental comfort while practicing yoga. Hence, clean, loose, free-flowing clothes; preferably cotton garments should be worn. In cold climates, a shirt or sweater can be worn. Jewellery and accessories should be avoided and practice with bare-feet to ensure contact with the Mother earth.

17. As the body has to be stretched in all directions, yogic practice has to be done on a clean mat, rug, carpet or a blanket.
18. You should practice Yoga on the ground. Never perform yoga on sofas and beds.

Types of Yoga

One of the features of yoga, which can be confusing at first, is that a variety of forms of yoga are practiced. Together, they are called Yoga. While these share common elements, some focus more on postures and breathing exercises, whereas others have a greater focus on meditation and spirituality. Each emphasizes a particular path that comprises a certain set of beliefs, practices, and rituals. Yoga forms constitute a ladder of sorts, from the "lowest" form of *Hatha* yoga, with its focus on physical postures and breathing techniques, to the "highest" form known as Raja, or "union by mental mastery."

Newer forms of hybrids of yoga are also proposed such as *Power yoga, Aerobics* etc. There are also variations of yoga depending on "the teacher that is being followed."

The most popular and authentic forms of yoga are:

- *Hatha Yoga ("The yoga of vitality'):* The Foundation of Yoga.

- *Bhakti Yoga:* The Yoga of Love and Devotion towards Almighty God.
- *Karma Yoga ("The yoga of action"):* The Yoga of Selfless Action.
- *Jnana/Gyan Yoga:* The Yoga of Wisdom.
- *Raja Yoga: Ashtanga* Yoga.
- *Mantra yoga:* The divine power of mantra for healing and enlightment.
- *Kundalini Yoga:* The enlightening/opening of spiritual power centers in form of CHAKRAS in the body.
- *Seva Yoga:* The selfless services! This is integral part of all the Yoga system.

Ashtanga Yoga: The Eight Limbs of Yoga

Ashtanga Yoga literally means "eight limbs of yoga." The second chapter of the Yoga Sutras of *Patanjali* contains information about these limbs. It comprises the basis of *Ashtanga* Yoga Philosophy.

1. The following are the 8 practices or limbs: *Yama (moral restraints/ethical disciplines):* Our relation to others.
2. *Niyama (observances/rules of conduct):* Our relation to ourselves.
3. *Asana (posture)*: relation to our body.
4. *Prāṇāyāma (breath expension)*: Our relation to our breath or spirit.

5. ***Pratyāhāra (sensory withdrawal):*** Our relation to our sense organs.
6. ***Dhāraṇā (concentration):*** Our relation to our mind.
7. ***Dhyāna (meditation)***: Moving beyond the mind.
8. ***Samādhi (meditative absorption):*** Deep realization and inner union.

The *Yamas,* the first limb, comprises five parts: *Ahimsā* (non-harming/non violence with mind, words and deeds), *Satya* (honesty with mind, words and deeds), *Asteya* (non-stealing with mind, words and deeds), *Bramacharya* (directing one's energy towards the Divine with mind, words and deeds), *Aparigraha* (non-possessiveness and non-attachment with mind, words and deeds).

The *Niyamas* the second limb, also comprises five aspects: *Sauca* (purity with mind, words and deeds), *Santoṣa* (contentment with mind, words and deeds), *Tapas* (austerity practices with mind, words and deeds), *Svādhyāya* (self-study, and the study of sacred texts), *Īśvara praṇidhāna* (surrender to the Divine, with mind, words and deeds).

The first four limbs are known as *"external yoga,"* and the last four limbs are referred to as *"internal yoga."* The fifth limb, *pratyāhāra,* is like a bridge between the external and internal limbs.

As students of yoga, we are able to actively practice the external limbs, while the internal limbs are the fruits of a sincere and continuous practice!

The final limbs of our practice are manifested through Divine Grace and arise spontaneously. More importantly, they are not mental states; rather can be brought about by our own individual efforts. They are granted to us as a gift when we surrender ourselves to something greater than us.

The eight limbs of yoga are interconnected and not separate steps along the path. Whether one starts by practicing the physical postures, breathe awareness, or mindfulness in the daily practice of the *yamas* and *niyamas*, each limb encourages growth in the others.

As the body becomes steady and at ease, the breath starts to come under control, and the mind begins to experience moments of clarity, and essential peace. As and when the body becomes steady and at peace, the breath starts coming into control and ultimately the mind begins to experience moments of clarity and the eternal peace.

- To find more details on Types of Yoga and *Ashtanga* Yoga please visit our website www.worldwelfaremission.org

Let's begin

Feel the Grace: Sit comfortably, close the eyes for a minute, feel the body as a whole and feel the grace of God flowing through you for about 15 seconds and think the following for another 15 seconds: "In Thy presence O Lord ! Filled with Thy Grace I am starting Yoga *Sadhna*. Grant me good health, energy and efficiency in life. I feel Thy Grace, Thy Divine Presence."

YOGASANA

I. Prayer with Om Chanting

Sit comfortably, relax your mind, spine erect, shoulder relaxed, both hands folded in yogic prayer posture. First inhale and exhale 3 to 5 times comfortably.

Now 3 to 5 times Om chanting: Every time we inhale through nose before chanting Om. Longer and deeper breath and exhale through mouth by chanting OM, as longer as possible. Focus 25% on O and 75% on Ma...

II. Toning up of the Body

Two minute tone up of the heart, blood vessels, arteries, veins and capillaries. This practice of toning up the body amounts to pressing the blood gently towards the heart. The procedure of pressing and releasing mentioned below should be such that the palm and fingers, while releasing the grip, do not lose contact with the body.

1. Assume a comfortable seated position. Press the top of the head with the palms and fingers of both hands

   and 'gradually' begin to press and release, moving the hand pressure forward over the face, reaching the neck and the chest.
2. Press the top of the head with the palms and fingers of both hands together and gradually begin to press and release, moving the hand pressure down over the back of the neck and coming around to the chest.
3. Grasp the finger tips of the right hand with the palm and fingers of the left hand so that the palm of the left hand is down. Gradually move the pressure upward along the arm reaching up to the shoulder and chest.
4. Grasp the finger tips of the right hand with the palm and fingers of the left hand so that the palm of the left hand is up, press and gradually move the pressure upward along the arm reaching up to the shoulder and chest.
5. Repeat movements 3 and 4 except that you grasp the left hand with the right hand.

6. With the tips of the middle fingers meeting horizontally at the navel, both hands on the abdomen, begin no press and release the abdomen, gradually moving the pressure up toward the chest.
7. Using both hands begin to press and release the middle of the back and ribs up toward the heart as far as you can reach.
8. Start now with the right foot. Grasp the top of the toes with the right had and the sole of the foot with the left hand and together press and release, gradually moving the hand pressure along the leg up to the waist, thereby pressing the whole of the area.
9. Repeat movement 8 with the left foot.

III. Self Love

Sit comfortably, relax your mind. Now embrace yourself warmly. Feel that you are meeting the best person on this planet. Feel like you are meeting your best friend, that is none other than your good self! You have been taking care of everyone around you but most of the time you ignored yourself. Now

Promise yourself that you will take good care of yourself always. This is a beautiful self healing and empowering process to recharge yourself every day with Love, Care and Respect.

IV. Butterfly Pose

- Sit in a position with your spine erect and your legs spread straight.

- Bend your knees and bring your feet towards your pelvis. The soles of your feet should touch each other.
- Grab your feet tightly with your hands. You may place your hands underneath your feet in order to get support.
- Make some effort to bring your heels as close to your groin as possible.
- Take a deep breath in. Breathing out, press your thighs and knees downward towards the floor. Make a gentle effort to keep pressing them downward.
- Start flapping both your legs up and down as a butterfly does with its wings. Start slow and gradually increase the speed. Continue to breathe normally.
- Slow down and then stop. Take a deep breath in and as you exhale, bend forward, keeping your chin up and spine erect.
- Press your elbows on your thighs or on your knees, pushing your knees and thighs closer to the floor.

- Feel the stretch in your inner thighs and take long, deep breaths, relaxing the muscles more and more.
- Take a deep breath in and bring the torso up.
- As you exhale, gently release the posture. Now, Straighten your legs in front of you and relax.

Benefits of the Butterfly Pose

- Stretches the inner thighs, groins and knees, improving flexibility in the groin and hip region
- Improves intestinal and bowel movement
- Provides relief from fatigue that may arise from long hours of standing or walking
- Gives comfort from menstrual discomfort and menopause symptoms
- Helps in smooth delivery if practised regularly until late pregnancy

Precautions of the Butterfly Pose

Like all poses, butterfly stretch can be adjusted in order to accommodate the individual needs of your body.

If you are suffering from a groin or knee injury, do not perform this asana unless you keep a blanket under your outer thighs for support. Do not perform this pose without the support of a blanket. Also, sciatica patients should either completely avoid the pose or sit on a cushion to raise the hips. If you have any lower back disorders, do the postures only while keeping the spine erected. Avoid rounding the spine by bending forward.

V. *Tadasana*

Tadasana or the Palm Tree Pose is considered as the most basic of all the yoga poses for a beginner.

This is usually the first pose that is taught in yoga classes and fitness studios. Not only that, but when you are performing a series of yoga positions (even in advanced classes), you usually begin with this *Tadasana*. Although this pose is normally very simple, you can push your limits when attempting it. *Tadasana* also has a stilling effect, which helps you better your overall yoga practice.

Steps: *Tadasana* Pose steps are as follows:

Step 1: Stand straight by keeping your feet flat on the ground and your heels slightly apart. The bases of your big toes should be touching. Do not put more weight on any of your feet; rather distribute it evenly on both your legs. You can accomplish this by lifting and spreading your toes. Keep on doing this till you feel that your weight is evenly distributed and you are completely balanced.

Step 2: Do not let your thigh muscles to loose without hardening your belly. Lift the insides of your ankles so slightly that your feet appear to be cupped. While lengthening your tailbone, turn the upper parts of the thighs slightly inwards and lift your pubis towards the navel.

Try to mentally connect your groin to your inner thighs and your torso through an imaginary energy line. This will help you maintain your balance while stretching.

Step 3: Extend your shoulder blades and arch them slightly towards the back. Keep them stretched and then slowly release them back, but while you are doing that, do not push your ribs forward. Lift your sternum slightly and bring your arms behind your torso.

Step 4: Bring the middle of your head directly in alignment with the middle of your pelvis, by keeping your chin parallel to the floor.

Soften your throat and eyes. Stay in this position for at least 30 seconds. Try to keep it for about a minute, if you can keep your balance for longer.

Continue to breathe easily.

Precautions: Though the *Tadasana* Pose is regarded as one of the easiest and relaxing poses, however there are some precautions that you must take while performing the mountain pose. Some of these are as follows:

- Performing this pose requires concentration, and therefore, it is best not to attempt it when you have a headache or suffer from persistent migraines
- You should also avoid performing this pose if you have insomnia or any other sleep related disorder because it can cause alertness and prevent you from sleeping easily

- This pose is also contraindicated for those who suffer from blood circulation problems such as faulty valves and low blood pressure.

Benefits to a specific Body Part

Since the anatomical focus of this pose is thigh, the body organ that gets maximum benefit out of this pose is thigh.

Moreover, since this is a gentle stretching and restive pose, the thigh muscles are stretched and toned when you perform it. Apart from the thighs, the pose also helps strengthen and tone the following body parts:

- Legs
- Knees
- Ankles
- Buttocks
- Lower abdomen
- Shoulders
- Neck

Therapeutic Applications

This pose has several therapeutic applications; however, it can be used to relax the pressures and symptoms experienced due to sciatica.

It can be really helpful for those pregnant ladies who are suffering from sciatica. Other therapeutic benefits of the mountain pose are:

- Good for body stress relief, Joint pains, constipation and other stomach related issues.

- *Tadasana* can also help you lessen the effects of flat feet.
- *Tadasana* helps you improve your posture.
- *Tadasana* bolsters the lower part of your body and load-bearing joints.
- *Tadasana* helps in the betterment of concentration and increases alertness.

VI. Kapalbhati Kriya

Steps:

- Sit in a comfortable crossed leg sitting posture,- *Sukhasana* or *Vajrasana* and keep your back straight. Rest your hands on the knees (using *Gyan mudra* or *Aadi mudra*).
- Exhale using a force so that your abdominal muscles contract to the maximum.
- These exhalations are similar to your breath outs, but they should be forceful.
- Make sure while exhaling, the air should be pushed out of your lungs by contracting the diaphragm.
- After exhalation again do inhalation, but this time without any effort. To do this just relax your lungs, they will automatically expand and fill with air.
- One cycle of *Kapalabhati kriya* include one deep inhalation, then forceful exhalation and an effortless inhalation. Gap between two exhalations should be one second, means in one minute there should be 60 strokes/exhalation.

- A learner can practice up to three rounds, each with 15 exhalations. Small breaks between each round are allowed. Gradually increase the timing of repetition up to 3 minutes to 5 minutes nonstop. To get rid of obesity you can practice *Kapalbhati* 10 to 20 minutes continuously (specially in winter) in morning and repeat in evening for fast result. Initially you may feel some strain in lower abdomen and lower back area but don't worry, gradually everything will be all right.
- Those who have high blood pressure, heart disease and asthma should practice *Kapalbhati kriya* very slowly, under proper guidance.

Benefits of *Kapalbhati Kriya*

- It helps in detoxifying your lungs and the respiratory tracks
- Purifies blood by boosting the supply of oxygen
- Helps in reducing belly fat, as it tones your abdominal muscles
- Usually it is practised before practising **yoga poses** and before meditation. This will improve your concentration, alertness and prevent your mind from unwanted thoughts
- Students practising this *Kriya* will have great results in their studies, because it increases the concentration and sharpness of their mind.

Kapalabhati pranayama is a very good breathing exercise which clears your lungs and stretches your abdominal muscles. Meaning of *Kapal* **in Sanskrit** (ancient Indian language) is Forehead and *Bhati* means Shining, which means *kapalabhati* procedure gives you a shining face and inner radiance. This *pranayama* must be practised by students, as it improves the sharpness and alertness of their mind.

VII. Bhastrika Pranayama

Position: Meditation Posture (like *Sukhasana, Bajrasana* or *Padmasana*)

Focusing Chakra: On the *Manipura* Chakra (Navel Chakra)

The word *"Bhastrika Pranayama"* is derived from a Sanskrit word *Bhastrika*, which means breathing like a bellows (**धौंकनी**). Bellows is a device for producing a strong current of air which was used to fan fire in Ancient days. In *Bhastrika Pranayama* our lungs are made to move with movements that is very much similar to the bellows. And this is the reason why the *Bhastrika Pranayama* is known as the 'bellows breath'. *Bhastrika* (bellow-breathing) is a powerful and energetic *Pranayama* in yogic breathing. In Ancient yogis they called this breathing exercise as "the yogic breath of fire". If you have done *Kapalbhati Kriya*, you must be knowing that in this asana, the focus happens to be

only on exhalation which is forced, short and quick. In this *Kriya*, inhalation is natural and passive.

During exhalation, we also force the belly towards our spine in a brisk movement.

While in the *Bhastrika Pranayama*, inhalation and exhalation both are forced. The movement of belly along with every breath is an optional variation. Simply put, *Bhastrika Pranayama* is nothing but complete inhaling and exhaling so that our body gets adequate amount of oxygen.

There are two different techniques for *Bhastrika Pranayama*. One is predicated on the classical approach given within the *Hatha* yoga *Pradipika.* The other is a modern and changed version of the technique and involves the movement of the arms and shoulders alongside the breath. Here we described the *Bhastrika Pranayama* according to *"Hathayog Pradipika".*

Steps of *Bhastrika Pranayama*

- Sit either on the *Sukhasana, Bajrasana* or *Padmasana* with eye closed.
- Take a deep breath in (inhale), filling the lungs with air.
- After that, gently breathe out.
- In this inhaling and exhaling should take the same length of time-2 to 5 seconds to breathe in and 2 to 5 seconds to breathe out.
- While you breathe in (inhale), assume that you are taking in positive energy and vibrations, and that you are being energized by them.

- During breathe out (exhale), imagine that you are taking out all the toxins from your body and mind. Feel that during breathe out all the toxins come out through your breathe.

Benefits of *Bhastrika Pranayama*

- This is intense purifying process.
- It gives strength to lungs.
- Helps in allergies, Asthma, reparatory diseases, Tonsil and Thyroid.
- Gives calmness to the mind.
- Brings the proper balance of three *Doshas—Vata, Pitta,* and *Kapha*
- Purifies the blood and kicks out the foreign objects and toxins form body.
- Our heart and head get adequate quantity of fresh and pure air by which our health is improved.
- Warms up our body.
- Helps prevent in common cold.
- It strengthens our immune system.
- *Bhastrika pranayama* is one of the best ways for gaining enlightenment and tranquility.

Precautions

People who are suffering from High blood pressure and acute heart problems should not be try this breath exercise.

VIII. *Naukasana* (Boat Pose)

The very name *Naukasana* is derived from a Sanskrit word *"Nauka"* which means "boat". So, the very term *Naukasana* means posture of a boat. This (boat pose) asana is extremely instrumental in curing a number of physical disorders.

Basically *Naukasana* helps to strengthen the lungs, liver and pancreas. It helps to increases the circulation of blood and maintains the sugar level. *Naukasana* is a posture in which our body takes the shape of boat. It makes circulation of blood and oxygen around abdomen and lower back at a much faster rate. *Naukasana* is good for those who wish to reduce belly and wants to develop abs muscles.

In this section, we discuss basic *Naukasana* pose, because other types of *Naukasana* is advanced in level. First of all do simple pose of *Naukasana,* Once you are perfect than go for advanced level of this Asana.

Steps for *Naukasana* (Boat pose)

- Lie on your back with your feet together and arms beside your body.
- As you exhale, take a deep breath in, lifting your chest and feet off the ground and stretching your arms towards your feet.

- Your eyes, fingers and toes should be in a line.
- Feel the tension in your navel area as the abdominal muscles contract.
- Keep breathing deeply and easily while maintaining the pose.
- Hold the position for few seconds.
- As you exhale, come back to the ground slowly and relax.
- Do this asana 3-4 times daily, but avoid an overdo.

Benefits of *Naukasana*

- Invigorates the back and abdominal muscles.
- Tones the leg and arm muscles.
- Very effective for the people with hernia.
- Helps removing belly fat.
- Improves digestion.
- Helps in developing six packs ABS.
- Improves the circulation of blood.
- Gives strength to thigh, hips, shoulders and neck.
- Regulates the function of liver, pancreas and lungs.
- Maintains the function of kidney, thyroid and prostate glands.

Precautions of the *Naukasana*

- Do not practice this yoga pose if you have low blood pressure, severe headache, migraine, or if you have suffered from some chronic diseases or spinal disorders in the recent past.

- Asthma and heart patients are advised to avoid this pose.
- Women should avoid doing Boat pose (*Naukasana*) during pregnancy and during the first two days of the menstrual cycle.

IX. *Dhanurasana*

The name *"Dhanurasana"* is derived from the Sanskrit words *Dhanura* which means "bow" and Asana means "posture" or "seat".

This body posture is named after the shape it takes-that of a bow. *Dhanurasana* is also sometimes linked with upward wheel pose or *Urdhva Chakrasana.* The Bow or *Dhanurasana* raises both halves of the body at once, combining the movements of the Cobra and Locust, and countering the Plough and the Forward Bend, same as an archer stringing a bow. In this you use your hands and arms to pull your trunk and legs up together to form a curve. It tones muscles and maintains the elasticity of spine, improving posture and increasing vitality.

Steps of *Dhanurasana*

- Lie on your stomach
- Hold your both feet with your hands in such a way so that you make a back bend and position like a bow.

- Pull your both feet slowly – slowly, as much as you can. Look straight ahead with a smile on your face.
- Keep the pose stable while witnessing your breath.
- After 1-20 seconds as you exhale, bring your legs and chest gently to the ground and relax.

Benefits of *Dhanurasana*

- *Dhanurasana* strengthens the back and the abdomen simultaneously.
- Keeps you active and energetic.
- Helps improve stomach disorders.
- Helps in reducing fat around belly area.
- Helps improve menstrual disorders and reproductive system in women.
- Helps regulate pancreas and hence is recommended for people with diabetes
- Expands the thoracic region of the chest
- Helps alleviate hunchback
- Increases appetite
- Bow Pose combines the benefits of the Cobra and the Locust postures.

Balancing the weight of the body on your abdomen also reduces abdominal fat and keeps the digestive and reproductive systems healthy. As this Asana necessitates balancing the weight of the body on abdomen, therefore it also helps in reducing abdominal fat and keeping the reproductive systems healthy.

Cautions

- Those who suffer from high blood pressure, back pain, headache, and migraine or, had a surgery recently, should not practice *"Dhanurasana"*.
- Ladies should not practice this during pregnancy and in periods.

Note: You should not perform these *Asanas* without the supervision of a yoga professional. In order to do *Dhanurasana* faultlessly, you will need to be expert in performing simple asanas. Do *Yogasana* as much as you can, but do not overlook your capabilities. And the most important thing: once you become perfect in basic *asanas*, then and only then go for the advance *Asanas*.

X. *Mandukasana* (Frog Pose)

The word *"Mandukasana"* is derived from a Sanskrit word *"Manduk"* which means frog. In this Asana, you have to make a pose of that of a frog. It is a very simple Asana and hence people of all age groups can perform it without any inconveniences or difficulties.

In Yoga there are so many variations in *Mandukasana*, but here we will know about two easiest methods to do *Mandukasana*.

Steps of *Mandukasana* (Frog Pose)

- Sit in *Vajrasana* (thunderbolt Pose)

- Close the fists of your both hands.
- While clinching the fists, press your thumb inside with the fingers.
- While pressing the navel with your both fists, exhale and bend forward.
- Hold the breath when you are in the position of bending forward and keep looking straight.
- Stay in this position for some time (hold the position as much as you can), inhale and come back to starting position (*Vajrasana*).
- Repeat this for three to four times.

Here is a second way or method to perform *Mandukasana* in simpler way. The steps of this method are as follows:

Steps of *Mandukasana* (Method–2)

- Sit in *Vajrasana.*
- Place your right palm on your left palm; keep them on the navel.
- Now press your stomach inwards.
- Exhale and bend forward (same as method 1); and keep looking straight.
- Hold your breath and position for some time.
- Slowly inhale and come back to Starting Position.
- Repeat this for 3 to 4 times.

Benefits of *Mandukasana*

- Increases the secretion of insulin and hence it is beneficial for diabetics.

- Cures the problems related to stomach.
- It is beneficial in cardiovascular diseases.
- Useful for flexibility of thighs and legs.
- Reduces extra fat from thighs and hips.
- It improves the functioning of digestive and excretory system.
- It cures the pain of ankles, knees and back.

Precaution: People who are having some abdominal injuries or suffering from back pain, knee injury, etc. should not perform this asana. It will be better if you take the advice of a yoga expert before performing this Asana.

XI. *Agnisar Pranayama*

Method of Practice

1. Sit in *Sukhsasana, Vajrasana* or *Padmasana* as per your convenience and keep the hands on the knees in a comfortable position. Close the eyes slightly and concentrate on the mind with normal breathing.
2. Exhale slowly, but deeply. Stop the breathe from outside, i.e., do *Bahirmukh*. Stretch both the hands straight and keep them on the knees with slight pressure. Contract and expand the stomach. Focus on touching the navel deep inside the stomach.
3. Keep the stomach and hands normal before doing *poorak* i.e., inhale. Now take deep, stable and slow breathe.
4. This is one of the cycles of *Agnisar pranayama*. In one cycle contract and expand the stomach at least

ten times. Increase the number to 30. Initially, practice it for 5 times and then slowly increase it up to 15 cycles. During winters, you can practice it for 25 cycles. Breathe normally, rest for sometimes and then perform *shavasana.*

Precautions during *Agnisar Pranayama*

1. This pranayama should be done in the morning hours after getting free from the morning chores. Those who want to practice it in the evening, should do after four hours of having lunch.
2. During winters, *Agnisar pranayama* should be done according to pre-defined procedures. This is the best time for this *pranayam.* During summers, ten rounds of *Shitali pranayama* should be definitely practised, after doing this *pranayama.*
3. During the practice period the person should eat simple, pure food. Avoid eating heavy, oily, fried and non- vegetarian food. If you consume alcohol or smoke, quit it completely.
4. The patients of intestinal problems, hernia, high blood pressure and other diseases should not practice it.
5. If you have undergone stomach operation recently then this *pranayama* should not be practised. It should be done under the guidance of some yoga expert after few months of your operation.
6. Stop the practice immediately if you experience tiredness. You may practice it the other day.

7. Practice it according to your physical capacity. Do not do *kumbhak* in excess of your body capacity. Make sure that during *Bahirkumbhak*, even the slightest air does not get inside.
8. Patients suffering with ear, nose and eye problems should not practice *agnisar pranayama.*

Benefits of *Agnisar Pranayama*

Agnisar pranayama increases the internal energy and gives vitality. Those who are suffering with constipation, indigestion and loss of appetite, will be benefitted with its regular practice. People with excessive fat on their stomach, can get rid of the fat, if they practice this Asana regularly.

This pranayama helps overcome laziness, disinterest and strengthens the internal organs, muscles, nerves and blood veins. People suffering with lung problems can gain a lot. This *pranayama* cures asthma, tuberculosis and several other diseases. It also cures the entire throat related problems like old *kapha* etc. It cures sleepiness and boosts inner energy.

XII. *Nadi Shodhan Pranayama* (Alternate Nostril Breathing Technique)

How to do Alternate Nostril Breathing *(Nadi Shodhana)*

- Sit in a comfortable position with the spine erected and the hips relaxed. Release any tension from your jaw. Close your eyes.

- Place your left hand on your left knee with the palm face upward, or in the Chin *Mudra* by pressing the index finger and thumb together.
- Place the tip of the index finger and middle finger of the right hand in between the eyebrows with the ring finger and little finger on the left nostril, and the thumb on the right nostril. Use the ring finger and little finger to open and close the left nostril and use the thumb for the right nostril.

- On an exhalation, close the right nostril with your thumb and breathe out through the left nostril.
- Breathe in through the left nostril and then close with the ring finger.
- Release the thumb on the right nostril and breathe out through the right nostril.
- Inhale through the right nostril, close with the thumb, release the ring finger from the left side and exhale through the left nostril.
- These two full breaths are known as one round of Alternate Nostril Breath.
- Perform 5 to 9 rounds of this alternating breath between the nostrils.
- Always inhale through the same nostril you just exhaled through.

The *Nadi Shodhana Pranayama,* apart from relaxing mind, does also prepare your mind and body for effective meditation. And this is the reason why people perform this Asana before performing meditation.

Benefits of Alternate Nostril Breathing *(Nadi Shodhana Pranayama)*

- Calms and centers the mind
- Brings the mind to the present moment (releasing old fears, regret, and worry)
- Therapeutic for the circulatory and respiratory systems
- Stress relieving and relaxing for the body and mind
- Helps harmonize the left and right hemispheres of the brain, which correlate to the logical and emotional sides of our personality.
- Helps purify and balance the *nadis*, the subtle energy channels, thereby ensuring smooth flow of *prana* (life force) through the body.
- Maintains body temperature.

3 Things to Remember When Practising *Nadi Shodhana Pranayam*

- The breathing pattern is breath out, breathe in, switch sides.
- Do not force the breath - keep it as gentle and natural as possible. Allow the breath to be smooth and devoid of any force or pressure.
- Place the fingers very lightly on the forehead and nose.

XIII. *Surya Namaskara*

Surya Namaskara is regarded as one of the most beneficial yogic Asanas for the human body. This Asana comprises *Yogasanas* and *Pranayama.*

It is Surya *Namaskar* consists of *Yogasanas* and *Pranayama.* The *Pranayama* and its advantages are skillfully incorporated in Surya *Namaskar.* The Mantras (*Bija Mantras*), which are chanted before practising, are also very useful.

In all this, Surya *Namaskar* is an appreciated exercise among people of all age groups. Surya *Namaskar* or Sun Salutation is the best way to burn the calories and reduce weight. This Asana is also recommended for obesity.

Step 1: In the whole, Surya *Namaskar* includes 12 different positions, they are:

Inhale and maintain the position as shown in picture in the standing position with hands joined together near chest and feet together.

Namaskar Mudra

Hasta parshwasana

Step 2: *Hastha Parshvasana*, Breathing in, bring the arms forward and up, and then while keeping the arms close to the ears, gently bend backward. Straighten the elbows and knees, and let the head drop back as comfortably as you can. While exhaling, maintain the normal sitting posture.

Step 3: Exhale and bend forward at the waist till palms touch the ground in line with the toes. Do not bend knees while performing. At first, you may find it difficult to attain the ideal position, but keep on trying to bend as much as possible without bending in the knees. (Person with lower back pain should avoid this posture).

Hasta padasana

Do's

While exhaling, bend forward at the waist.

Palms touching the ground, fingers pointing forward, thumbs at 90 degree angle.

Legs straight.

Try to touch the forehead to the knees (please do it comfortably, it may take time to achieve the actual position. Do not give any jerk).

Relax the neck.

Don'ts

- Do not bend the knees.
- Do not keep the neck tight.

Step 4: Inhale and take the right leg back with right toes on the floor, press the waist downwards and raise the neck, stretch the chest forward and push shoulders backwards. Ensure that your both hands and left leg is in the same position. Keep the left leg folded.

Ashwa Sanchalana

Do's

Take the left leg backwards and touch the knee to the floor, keeping the toes erect.

The knee of the right leg should be bent

The knee of the left leg should touch the ground

Drop the waist/hips towards the floor

Gaze upwards, with both your arms straight

Don'ts

- Make sure that your neck does not bend forward.
- You should not bend the elbows.

Step 5: Holding your breath raise the knee of your left leg. Take the right leg backwards and keep it close to the left leg. Straighten both your legs and hands. Keep the neck straight and site fixed. Keep both the toes erect. Make sure that your neck, spine, thighs and the feet are in a straight line.

Dandasasana

Do's

Take the right leg back and place it beside the left leg, keeping the toes erect.

Keep the body in one straight line — plank position.

Keep your arms straight.

Gaze forward.

Don'ts

- Do not bend the arms
- Do not look downward
- Do not bend the hips/waist towards the floor
- Do not stick the buttocks into the air
- Do not bend the knees

Step 6: Breathing out, bend both the hands and elbows and touch chin or forehead on the ground. Now, touch the knees on the ground, keep both the elbows close to chest. The chin/forehead, chest, both the palms, toes, knees should touch the ground, but rest of the body should not touch the floor. Since only eight parts rest on the ground, hence it is known as' *Ashtanga Pranam'* position.

Ashtanga Pranam

Do's

Bring the body towards the floor, placing the 8 parts on the floor: Toes, knees, chest, palms, and chin/forehead.

Keep the hands close to the body, next to the shoulders.

Keep the elbows pointed to the sky and close the body.

Don'ts

- Make sure that your thighs, hips, waist or abdomen do not touch the floor.
- Do not allow your elbows to fall away from the body.

Step 7: Inhale and straighten the elbows, stretch the shoulders upwards and press the waist downwards, without bending the arms. Keep the knees and toes on the floor. Push the neck backwards and look upwards.

Bhujangasana

Do's

Push the upper body upwards so that your arms do not bend.

Make sure that your fingers get pointed forwards, palms on the ground and thumbs at 90 degree angle.

Open the chest and pull the shoulders downwards.

Drop the head and neck backwards and look upwards.

Hold your heels, legs and knees together.

Keep your toes erect.

Don'ts

- Do not let your legs or heels separated
- Do not bend the elbows
- Do not bend and forward your shoulders towards the ears

Step 8: Hold the breath, bend the neck downwards and press the chin in the throat, push the body backwards and touch the heels on the ground, raise the waist upwards, do not move the palms on the floor.

Bhu dharasana or Parvatasana

Do's

Push the body upward so that your buttocks and waist are raised, thereby giving your body an Inverted 'V' position.

Take the head and chin towards the chest

Try to touch the heels to the floor

Don'ts

- Make sure that your knees do not bend
- Do not bend the arms

Step 9: Hold the breath as in position 7, bring the right leg in the front and place it in between the hands like in position 3. But, instead of left leg in the front, here take right leg and place left leg in the back with left knee and toes on the ground.

Ashwa sanchalana

Do's

Take the right leg forward and place it between the hands.

The knee of the right leg will be bent.

The knee of the left leg should touch the ground.

Bend the waist/hips towards the floor.

Look to the sky, with both your arms straight.

Don'ts

- Make sure that your neck does not bend forward.
- Do not bend the elbows.

Step 10: Breathing out, bring the left leg forwards as in the position 2 and place it in between both the arms.

Hasta Padasana

Do's

Take the left leg forward and place it beside the right.

Palms should touch the ground, fingers should be pointed forward and your thumbs should be straight.

Legs straight.

Try to touch the forehead to the knees, relax the neck.

Don'ts

- Make sure that your knees do not bend.
- Do not keep the neck tense.

Step 11: As in Step 2: *Hasta parshwasana*

1. *Hastha Parshvasana*, Stand in comfortable pose, entwine your fingers behind the back and inhale and stretch the chest forward and hands backwards.
2. Simultaneously stretch your neck slightly backwards, hold for few seconds.

3. And Breathing outcome back to the normal standing posture.

Step 12: While inhaling, start getting up and come to the position as it is in position 1.

Benefit and precautions: *Surya-namaskar* is a complete Asana for overall fitness of the mind and body. This Asana is performed to strengthen and activate all organs and endocrine system. You can repeat this asana 2 to 10 times according to the availability of time and convenience.

Person with back pain, Hernia, Appendicitis, High blood pressure and Heart disease should avoid doing *Surya-namaskar.*

XIV. *Paschimottanasana*

- Sit up with the legs stretched out straight in front of you, keeping the spine erect and toes flexed towards you.

- Inhale and raise both arms above your head and stretch up.
- Exhale and bend forward from the hip joints, chin moving toward the toes. Keep the spine erect focusing on moving forwards towards the toes; do not move downwards towards the knees.

- Place your hands on your legs, wherever they reach, without putting any pressure. If you can, take hold of your toes and pull on them to help you go forward.
- While inhaling, lift your head slightly and straighten your spine.
- While exhaling, gently move the navel towards the knees.
- Repeat this movement two or three times.
- Drop your head down and breathe deeply for 20-60 seconds.
- Stretch the arms out in front of you.
- While inhaling, come back up to the sitting position with the strength of your arms.
- Now, exhale and lower the arms.

XV. *Pawan Muktasana*

1. Lie on your back with your feet together and arms beside your body.
2. Breathe in and as you exhale, bring your right knee towards your chest and press the thigh on your abdomen with clasped hands.

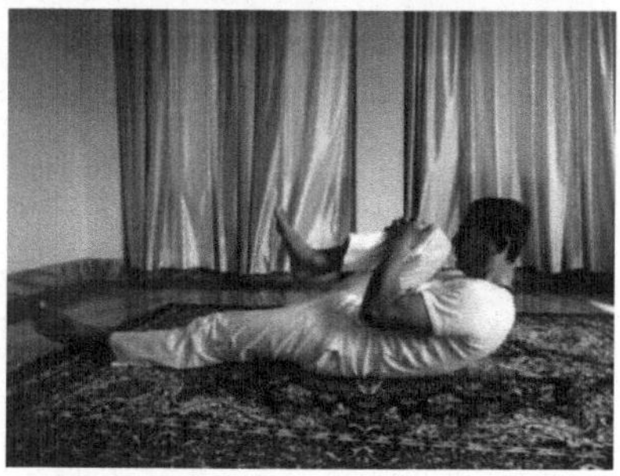

3. Breathe in again and as you exhale, lift your head and chest off the floor and touch your chin to your right knee.

4. Hold it there, as you take deep, long breaths in and out.

5. Checkpoint: As you exhale, tighten the grip of the hands on the knee and increase the pressure on the chest. As you inhale, loosen the grip.
6. As you exhale, come back to the ground and relax.
7. Repeat this pose with the left leg and then with both the legs together.
8. You may rock up and down or roll from side to side 3-5 times and then relax.

Benefits of the Wind-Relieving Pose (*Pawan Muktasana*)

1. Back and abdominal muscles become strong.
2. Leg and arm muscles get strength
3. The intestines and other organs in the abdomen get more strength
4. Digestion becomes easier and release of gas speeds up
5. Blood circulation in the hip joints enhances and tension in the lower back reduces significantly

Precautions of the Wind-Relieving Pose (*Pawan Muktasana*)

1. Avoid practising Wind-Relieving Pose (*Pawan Muktasana*) if you are facing the following health

issues: high blood pressure, heart problem, hyperacidity, hernia, slip disc, testicle disorder, menstruation, neck and back problems, and after the second trimester of pregnancy.

XVI. *Uttanapadasana*

Position

1. Lie on your back.
2. Do your feet together.
3. Place palms facing down to the floor at your side 4 to 6 inches away from the trunk.

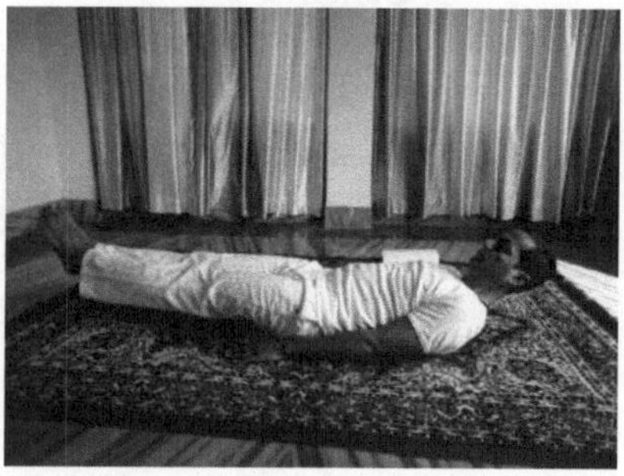

Steps

1. Inhale and lift both legs to 30 degrees.
2. Hold your breath in the posture as much as you can.
3. Exhale and bring your legs down to the floor without bending your knees.
4. Again inhale and raise the legs to 60 degrees.
5. Hold your breath for a while.
6. Exhale and bring the legs down to the ground.
7. You can perform *Ardha-Uttanapadasana* in the same manner, by lifting your one leg at a time.

Time: Repeat up to three times for up to five minutes, and then increase the duration as per your convenience and the availability of time.

Precautions

1. Make sure that your legs are straight during lifting and bringing your leg.
2. While lifting or lowering your legs down, avoid any sudden or jolting movement.
3. This posture is not for those who are suffering from high blood pressure, backache or any heart related problems.

Benefits: This posture reduces obesity and abdominal disorders, and increases the speed of blood circulation in the body. It does also help overcome constipation.

NATURE CURE

I. Kunjal

Kunjal means an elephant. In this process, one takes in water like an elephant and throws out quickly. This process is very simple. *Kunjal* process is also called *Gajakarni.*

Steps: In the early morning, clean your teeth, finish your natural call and on empty stomach

1. Drink 8 to 10 glasses, approximately one and half to two liters of tepid water having half a teaspoonful of salt added to water. Take 7 to 8 glasses quickly.
2. When you take in 7 or 8 glasses of water, the same will come out of belly by itself (automatically). In case this does not occur, take four fingers of your right hand right up to the inside of the throat and all water will be belched out. This will clean inside of neck, food pipe and stomach. This cleaning is very essential for asthmatic, acidity and diabetic patients.

Do not try to take in only 2 or 3 glasses full of water and force the water out by effort, because if the color of water seems slightly red due to friction in neck there can be unnecessary doubt of blood having been thrown out.

If a little water still retains in the stomach, it will get out forcibly through urine.

Strong acid gets washed out due to this process and one saves oneself from getting ulcer.

Precautions

There is no risk in carrying out *Kunjal* process. But those who have very high blood pressure, heart issues, weakness, during pregnancy, should avoid this *kriya.*

Do not either eat or drink anything at least for a period of one hour after this process. You will feel much hunger after one hour, than you should take food, which will not spoil your digestive system.

II. Naturopathy

Naturopathy for diabetes: Diabetes results from the lack of adequate secretion of insulin by pancreas, which puts adverse effect in carbohydrate metabolism and the metabolism of protein and fast. Type 2 diabetes is the most common type of diabetes, while type 1 is also not a rare phenomenon. The body of a diabetic is characterised by an abnormally elevated level of blood sugar as well as excretion of excess glucose through urine. But, the good thing is that nature has the power to control diabetes at the earliest.

- Mud Therapy is beneficial for hyperglycemic patients.
- Hydrotherapy: Hot and Cold Fomentation over abdomen, Cold hip bath, Hot and cold hip bath, Wet abdomen pack, spinal bath. All these form an important part of treatment. Enema thoroughly cleansed the colon and helps the bowel to assume normal characteristics.
- Bathing in cold water greatly increases the circulation and enhances the capacity of the muscles to utilize sugar.
- Massage Therapy helps to energizes and revitalizes the whole body.
- Sun Bath: Water kept in brown bottle and exposed to sun rays for at least 8 hours in half cup, dose twice a day after meal is also found beneficial.
- Exercise, especially morning walk and Yoga is good remedies diabetic patients
- For Naturopathy and Yoga treatment always select a good center nearby. Never try everything on your own.

III. Hip Bath

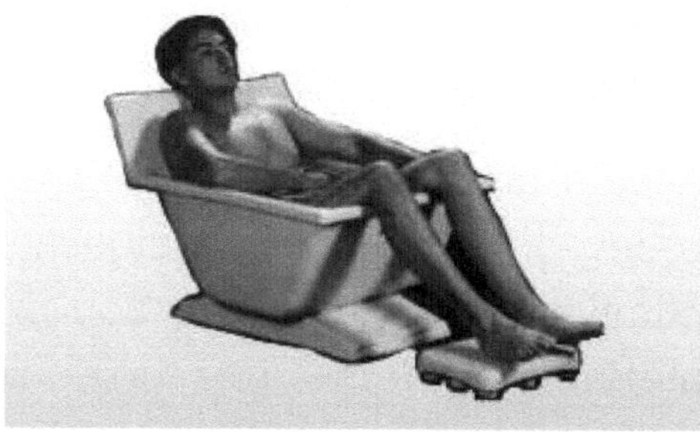

The hip bath is regarded as one of the most important forms of hydrotherapy. As the name suggests, this mode of treatment pertains to only the hips and the abdominal region below the navel. A special type of tub is used for this purpose. The tub is filled with water in such a way that it covers the hips and reaches up to the navel when a person sits in it. Unusually, four to six gallons of water are required. A common tub may also be used in case any special tub is not available. A support may be placed under one edge to elevate it by two or three inches. Hip bath is given in cold, hot, neutral or alternate temperatures.

IV. Cold Hip Bath

The water temperature should be 100C (10 degreeC) to 180(18 DegreeC). Though the duration of the bath is usually 10 minutes, but it may vary from one minute to 30 minutes in some specific conditions.

If the patient feels cold or is very weak, a hot foot immersion should be given with the cold hip bath.

The patient should rub the abdomen briskly from the navel downwards and across the body with a moderately coarse wet cloth. The legs, feet and upper part of the body should remain completely dry during and after the bath. The patient should undertake moderate exercise like *Yogasanas*, after the cold hip bath, to warm the body.

Benefits

A cold hip bath is a routine treatment in most diseases. It relieves constipation, indigestion, obesity and helps the eliminative organs to function properly. It is also helpful in uterine problems like irregular menstruation, chronic uterine infections, pelvic inflammation, piles, hepatic congestion, chronic congestion of the prostate gland, seminal weakness, impotency, sterility, uterine and ovarian displacements, dilation of the stomach and colon, diarrhea, dysentery, hemorrhage of the bladder and so on. The cold hip bath should not be employed in acute inflammations of the pelvic and abdominal organs, ovaries and in painful contractions of the bladder, rectum or vagina.

V. Hot Hip Bath

This bath is usually taken for eight to 10 minutes at a water temperature of 400C (40 DegreeC) to 450(45 DegreeC). The bath should start at 400(40 Degree)C. The temperature should be gradually increased to 450C (45 DegreeC). No friction should be applied to the abdomen. The practising person should drink one glass of cold water before entering the tub. A cold compress should be placed on the head.

Benefits

A hot hip bath helps to relieve painful menstruation, pain in the pelvic organs, painful urination, inflamed rectum or bladder and painful piles. It also benefits enlarged prostatic gland, painful contractions or spasm of the bladder, sciatica, neuralgia of the ovaries and bladder. A cold shower bath should be taken immediately after the hot hip bath.

Precautions: Proper care should be exercised to prevent the practising person from catching a chill after the bath. The bath should be terminated if the person feels giddy or complains of excessive pain.

VI. Neutral Hip Bath

The temperature of the water should be 320(32 degree)C to 360(36 degree)C. Here too, friction to the abdomen should be avoided. This bath is generally taken for 20 minutes to an hour. The neutral hip bath helps to relieve all acute and sub-acute inflammatory conditions such as acute catarrh of the bladder and urethra and sub acute inflammations in the uterus, ovaries and tubes. It also relieves neuralgia of the fallopian tubes or testicles, painful spasms of the vagina and prorates of the anus and vulva. In addition to these, it is a sedative treatment for erotomania (a delusion in which a person believes that another person (typically of higher social status) is in love with him or her. in both sexes.

VII. Alternate Hip Bath

This is also known as revulsive hip bath. The temperature in the hot tub should be 400C(40 degree) to 450(45 degree)C and in the cold tub 100(10 degree)C to 180(18 degree)C. The patient should alternately sit in the hot tub for five minutes and then in the cold tub for three minutes. The duration of the bath is generally 10 to 20 minutes. The head and neck should be kept cold with a cold compress. The treatment should end with a dash of cold water to the hips.

Benefits

This bath relieves chronic inflammatory conditions of the pelvic viscera such as salpingitis, ovaritis, cellulitis and various neuralgias of the genito-urinary organs, sciatica and lumbago.

Precautions

Certain precautions need to be taken while taking a therapeutic bath like alternate hip bath. Full baths are prohibited within three hours after a meal and one hour before a meal. However, local baths, such as hip bath and foot bath can be taken, two hours after a meal. Clean and pure water is a must for the bath and water once used for this purpose, should not be reused.

While taking baths, temperature and duration should be strictly observed to obtain the desired effects. A thermometer should always be used to measure the temperature of the body. Women should not take any of the baths during menstruation. They can take only hip baths during pregnancy till the completion of the third month.

VIII. Mud Therapy

Mud is one of five elements of nature having immense impact on the body, both in wellness and illness.

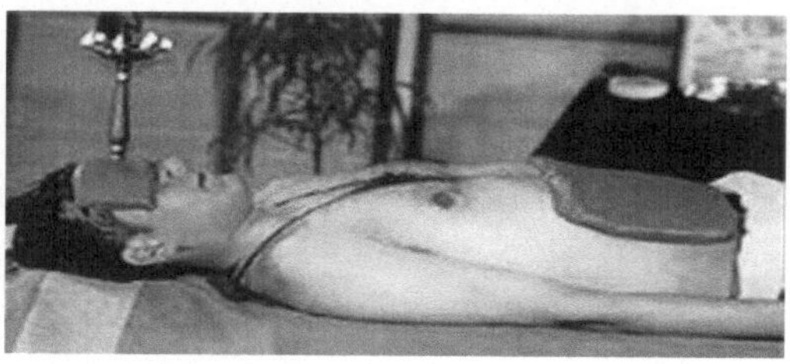

Though in mud therapy, mud is needed, but that mud should not have any semblance of stones, grass particles or any other such impurities. So, before using it for therapy, make sure that it does not have any impurity.

Here mud is applied to the whole body. The mud helps in restoring the perfect blood circulation and metabolism rate that tends to get affected with increased sugar levels in the blood.

Mud therapy is very simple and effective treatment modality. The mud used for this should be clean and taken from 3 to 4 ft. depth from the surface of the ground. There should be no contamination of stone pieces or chemical manures etc. in the mud.

Benefits of mud

1. Its black color absorbs all the colors of the Sun and conveys them to the body.
2. Mud retains moisture for a long time. It causes cooling when it is applied over the body. Its shape and consistency can be changed easily by adding water.
3. It is easily available.

Mud Pack-Local Application

Keep soaked mud in a thin, wet muslin cloth and make it into a thin flat brick depending on the size of the patient's abdomen and apply it. The duration of the mud pack application is 20 to 30 minutes. When applied in cold weather, place a blanket over the mud pack and cover the body as well.

Benefits of mud therapy

1. When applied to abdomen, it relieves all forms of indigestion. It is effective in decreasing intestinal heat and stimulates peristalsis.

2. A thick mud pack applied to head in congestive headache relieves the pain immediately. Hence, this is recommended whenever there is necessity for a prolonged cold application.
3. Application of the pack is recommended in cases of conjunctivitis, hemorrhages in the eyeball, itching, allergy, etc. It does also help rectify the errors of refraction like short sight and long sight and glaucoma where it helps to reduce eyeball tension.

सर्वे भवन्तु सुखिनः सर्वे सन्तु निरामया सर्वे भद्राणि
पश्यन्तु मा कश्चित् दुःखभाग् भवेत्

May all be happy May all be free from sorrow!
May all be prosperous May no-one be unhappy!!

Programs conducted by Acharya Krishna Deo

Program Pictures: 'Sahaj Krishna Yog Sadhana Shivir'
Conducted by Acharya Krishna Deo

At Hotel Leela Palace New Delhi

DIET PLAN

Diet Therapy

Diet Therapy is also a part of Naturopathy.

Yoga + proper diet will give you 100% result!

We must adopt

1. Proper Diet.
2. Yoga, Walk & Meditation.
3. Stress Management/ Lifestyle Management.

(We take special sessions/Seminars/Corporate workshops on above topics. Contact us for details).

Here I am giving a general nature care diet plan for Diabetic patients.

(We have special/customized nature care diet plan services available for different age groups and body requirements. Throughout the world, by courier, email or at our clinic. Contact us for details).

Diet Plan Chart

1. Glasses of lukewarm water, after getting up in the morning.
2. **After washroom:** 10 Basil Leaves (*Tulsi Patta*) + one teaspoon fresh ginger juice. After half an hour,
3. **Morning Breakfast:** Raw seasonal and local fruits of different colors, between 6 am to 12 pm.
4. **Quantity:** Total body weight x 10 grams. Suppose your body weight is 70kgs, which means 70wgt x 10gms = 700 grams. You can have some dry fruits as well.
5. **Afternoon:** Two glasses of fresh mix vegetable juice (in one go or in breaks). After one hour 20 ml wheat grass juice or one teaspoon wheat grass powder with 250ml lukewarm water. After half an hour one teaspoon of Flax seeds (Alsi seed) soaked about 4 hrs.
6. **Lunch:** Vegetable juice- one or two glasses. Salads- Local and seasonal raw vegetables including leaves.
7. **Quantity:** Total body weight x 05 grams. Suppose your body weight is 70, which means 70wgt x 5gms= 350 grams. +Nuts.
8. **Dinner:** Fresh Sprouts (total body weight x 05gms).

Do's and Don'ts

- Everyday Half an hour to one hour walk or Yoga in proper guidance (including *Kapal Bhati*, 5 minutes

Agnisar, 5 minutes *Anuloma Viloma Pranayama* etc). Also meditate for 20 minutes morning and evening. Try to read or hear *Bhagwad Gita* everyday.

- For salad or vegetable juice you can select seasonal: Bottle-gourd (*Ghiya*), Tomato, Cucumber, Mint leaves, Carrot, Lettuce (*salad patta*), Emblica, Coriander leaves, Winter Melon(*Safed Petha*). Please do not add sugar or salt in anything.
- Have patience, chew your food properly, so that it takes the liquid form in your mouth mixed with *sliva*.
- **Everyday your ideal water intake should be**: Total weight divided by 10 minus 2. So any time you feel hungry and thirsty in between this diet, you can have lemon mixed lukewarm water. This is required for natural flushing and detoxification! (Or take water as prescribed by your family physician).
- Any kind of intoxication (Alcohol, Tobacco or smoking). Avoid milk products, meat, eggs, tea-coffee, (green tea is okay) cold drinks, Maida, sour or packaged food, onion and radish. **Love and respect yourself!**
- You can share your weekly health and weight updates in first month, there after monthly updates.
- We wish you a very very happy, healthy and prosperous life!

At Hotel Leela

Meditation Workshop

Received 'Yog Ratna' national award

MEDITATION

Choose any one meditation at one time

Meditation Basics

Meditation is the nature friendly way to retreat the mind, body and the human soul. It is not only responsible to provide the medium to nourish the body and mind, but also strengthens the soul. As meditation comprises series of practices focusing on visual objects, sounds and parts of the body or universe, it is advised to practice meditation under the guidance of some expert, Meditation Guru or Meditation Teacher. In the website worldwelfaremission.org you can explore the different meditation techniques and benefits of the meditations along with the cure of basic human diseases. Ayurvedic treatments are also followed by the certain meditation techniques.

Benefit of Meditation

As part of the research conducted in medical science various results came out like:

- It reduces heart diseases.
- It reduces various allergies of an individual.
- It also helps in blood pressure problem.
- It has shown improvement in concentration and the mental capabilities of an individual
- It reduces pain and increases emotional stability.
- People suffering from sleeping problems have noticed significant improvements after adopting meditation in their daily life.
- Problems like asthma and depression can also be cured.
- It reduces stress and brings calmness inside you.
- When this free of cost medicine are having so many benefits then why not we should start with it.

Sahaj Kundalini Meditation (Active Mantra Meditation to relax the hyperactive mind)

Steps:

1. Sit comfortably in *Sukhasana* (crossed legged).
2. Take five soothing breath longer and deeper.
3. Left hand in *Gyan mudra*.
4. Right hand touching the bottom of your spine (*Mooladhara Chakra*). Three or five *om* chanting here.

5. Now sift your right hand above one and half centimeter above *Mooladhara chakra*. Here, chant Om three to five times. This is *Swadhishthan Chakra* awakening.
6. Now, put your right hand on your navel. Here, chant Om three to five times.. This center is *Manipura Chakra* awakening.
7. Now put your right hand on the middle of your chest, parallel to your heart. Here, chant Om three to five times. This is *Anahata Chakra* awakening.
8. Now put your right hand on your throat. Here, chant Om three to five times. This center is *Vishuddhi Chakra* awakening.
9. Now put your right hand on your forehead. Here, chant Om three to five times. This center is *Agya Chakra* awakening. *Agya chakra* is between the eyebrows.
10. Now right hand on the top of your head. Here, chant Om three to five times.. This center is *Sahatrar Chakra* awakening.
11. Now you can lie dawn to relax or you can continue in sitting posture for 10 minutes. Simply observe your breath, heart beat or your stomach. Relax your mind and body.

- It may take about 20 minutes. But result is amazing. Please do it and experience it.
- **Timings:** Any time empty or light stomach. Morning and evening meditation is always ideal.

- Yogic Relaxation and simple meditation (Sahaj Krsna Meditation).

I. Witness your breath (*Shwas Preksha* or *Anapan Sati*):

- Sit comfortably in *Shukhasana* till the time you are comfortable and after sometime when you feel like

lying dawn you can continue this meditation in laying posture as well.

- We need to start this Asana by taking a few slow and deep breath with a feeling that there is peace and tranquility in each breath and then exhale with a feeling that stress, tension, worry and irritation are getting released. While concentrating, we should not entertain any thought, no matter how urgent or important a given thought is. We should rather witness our breathe effortlessly and naturally.
- Do not force your mind to concentrate; try to make it as simple and effortless as possible.
- After some time you may feel pure blankness of mind, enjoy this calmness and and peace within.
- If your mind is still flickering here and there, don't worry, give a smile to yourself and to bring back your awareness to your breathing, you can have

three to five longer and deeper breath. And then continue witnessing your natural breathing. Witness the touch of the breath within nose, the sensation of the breath, length of the breath, warmness or coldness of the breath, simply witness with neutral mind.

- Practice this every day and you will feel the calmness and satisfaction within yourself.
- Timings: 10 to 20 minutes.

II. Witness your stomach (*Udar Preksha*)

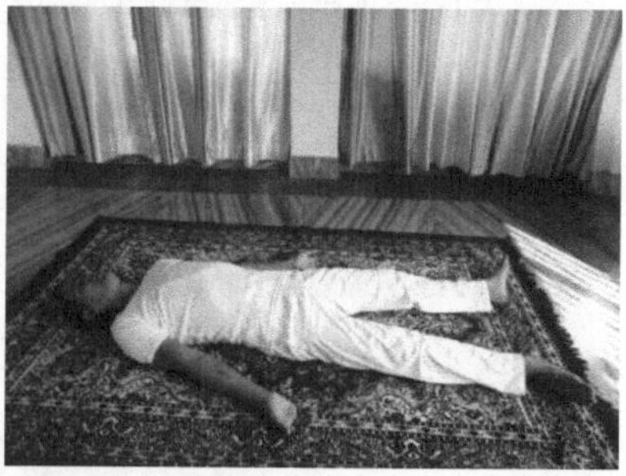

1. Sit comfortably in *Shukhasana* till the time you are comfortable and after sometime when you feel like lying dawn you can continue this meditation in laying posture as well.
2. We have to start this Asana by taking a few slow but deep breath with a feeling that there is peace and silence in each breath and then exhale with a feeling that stress, tension, worry and irritation are getting released. While concentrating, we should not entertain any thought, regardless of its urgency.
3. If some thoughts are coming, we should try to concentrate the 'stomach movement' effortlessly, naturally.

4. Don't force your mind to concentrate, try to make it simple and effortless as much as possible.
5. After some time you may feel pure blankness of mind, enjoy this calmness and and peace within.
6. If your mind is still flickering here and there, don't worries, give a smile to yourself and to bring back your awareness to your stomach movement, you can have three to five longer and deeper breath. And then continue witnessing your navel area. Witness, how naturally your stomach is bulging up and coming dawn by the rhythmic movement of your breath. Simply witness with neutral mind.
7. Practice this every day and you will feel the calmness and satisfaction within yourself.
8. Timings: 10 to 20 minutes.

III. *Vipassana* Meditation

In mantra and breath meditation, you focus on a word or your breath and try to empty your mind of everything else. This mental clearing is what most people mean when they refer to meditation.

But there's another kind of meditation, a practice Buddhists call *vipassana* or sometimes called mindfulness, or insight meditation. It is the art of becoming deeply aware of the present instant. Mindfulness means fully experiencing what happens in here and now. It is the art of focusing our minds on what's happening in and around us at this very moment. Mindfulness helps you turn down all the noise in your head- the guilt, anger, doubts, and uncertainties that upset us moment to moment. It is a technique that encourages you to stop and smell the roses.

The key is not so much what you focus on but how you do it. What is more important is the quality of the awareness you bring to each moment. That awareness should be meditative in the sense of being a silent witness, accepting - all without being judgmental. It teaches acknowledgment of the moment-to-moment reality and prepares those who use the technique to respond to that reality less impulsively and more effectively.

There are two kinds of mindful meditation - formal and informal. Yoga is a good example of the formal type. In a yoga class, participants focus intently on their *breathing* and the *postures,* moving slowly from one position to the next, exquisitely aware of their feelings during the process. Practitioners are taught to concentrate on their breathing and its passage through the body as they dismiss any distracting thoughts. Though it sounds simple, mindfulness takes practice, and the longer you practice, the easier the process becomes. Breathing is the vehicle of transition from our conventional, anxiety-ridden, goal-oriented experience of stressful living into a natural state of functional calm and tranquility. Tai chi offers a similar dimension of mindfulness. Informal mindfulness involves turning the headlong rush of daily living into a collection of discrete moments of experience, each savored fully. For example, we hand each of our students a single raisin and asks them to eat it. Ordinarily people would simply pop the raisin in their mouths, chew a few times and swallow, largely unconsciously. But mindful, meditative raisin eating is much different. It begins with looking intently at the raisin (*Munakka/Kismis*), considering its shape, weight, color and texture. Next comes placing the raisin in the mouth, focusing on how it feels on the tongue as the mouth welcomes it with salivation. Then the mindful raisin-eater chews the raisin slowly and thoroughly, focusing on its taste and texture. Finally, swallowing the raisin involves following it all the way down to the stomach. This meditation teaches us to live in present and enjoy every moment!

Once you commit to a mindfulness trigger-such as hanging up the phone, sipping a cup of tea or eating fruit snacks, starting the car or petting your dog-it is not difficult to work a dozen mindful moments into each day.

IV. Body Scan Meditation

Body Scan Meditation is often used by people who want to try a more formal type of mindfulness without attending a yoga or tai chi class.

1. Lie on your back with your legs uncrossed, your arms at your sides, palms up, and your eyes open or closed, as you wish.
2. Focus on your breathing, how the air comes in and goes out of your body.
3. After several deep breaths, as you begin to feel comfortable and relaxed, direct your attention to the toes of your left foot. Tune into any sensations in that part of your body while remaining aware of your breathing. It often helps to imagine each breath flowing to the spot where you're directing your attention. Focus on your left toe for one to two minutes.

4. Then shift your focus to the sole of your left foot and hold it there for a minute or two while continuing to pay attention to your breathing.
5. Follow the same procedure as you move to your left ankle, calf, knee, thigh, hip and so on all around the body.
6. Pay special attention to any areas that cause pain or are the focus of any medical condition (for asthma, the lungs; for diabetes, the pancreas).
7. Pay special attention to the head: the jaw, chin, lips, tongue, roof of the mouth, nostrils, throat, cheeks, eyelids, eyes, eyebrows, forehead, temples and scalp.
8. Eventually, focus on the very top of your hair, the uppermost part of your body. Then let go of the body altogether, and in your mind, hover above yourself as your breath reaches beyond you and touches the universe.
9. Repeat this Asana till the time stiffness and pain is not removed totally.

V. *Yog Nidra* in *Shavasana*

Steps:

1. Lie flat on the back, feet comfortably apart, arms and hands extended about 6" away from the body, palms facing upwards with half-folded fingers.
2. Close your eyes and gently relax your feet, keeping them completely still. Then relax your knees, chest and the arms. Keep both your hands still to achieve a relaxed position. Concentrate next on the head.

Move it gently to the side, let it rest and keep it free of all thoughts.

3. Now, concentrate the mind on rhythmic breathing. Breathing should be as slow and effortless as possible. Thus, all parts of the body are loosened to create a state of complete relaxation, which should be maintained for 10 to 15 minutes.

Benefits and Precautions

Shavasana is regarded as one of the most effective *asanas* to bring down high blood pressure (arterial hypertension). Therefore, any individual who cannot perform any other *Asanas* due to high blood pressure can perform can perform this Asana. This Asana is also performed by those who want to get immense relief to their mind. In addition to these benefits, this Asana does also help ease tension and stress to those who do lots of physical activities. This asana should be performed after completing the daily round of yogic *asanas. Shavasana* done during fasting soothes the nervous system. Everyone should attempt this asana.

TIPS ON SLEEP DISORDERS (INSOMNIA)

A sleepless night is worse than any other problem! Yes, a lack of good-quality sleep gives rise to a number of problems besides causing tiredness, poor concentration, and lethargy throughout the day, often throwing the life out of gear. An uninterrupted sleep of 7-8 hours is a must to maintain a healthy body and mind.

Good sleep also helps in yielding positive results in every task.

Tips that will guide you to have a good night's sleep regularly!

- Sleep is an essential aspect of any health program. You need sleep so that your body can repair itself, build muscle and burn fat.
- Bedroom must have a good environment so that it can induce sleep and prevent any kind of sleep disturbances. It must be dark, clean and with proper ventilation facilities.

- Your bed must have the right amount of blankets and soft pillows.
- A comfortable pillow and mattress are very essential not only to facilitate a good sleep, but also for your posture.
- Keep your bedroom at a comfortable temperature; it should be neither too warm nor too cold.
- You can also minimize noise and light during sleep by using ear plugs and window blinds.
- Try to keep your bedroom light dim.
- If you must sleep during the day, hang dark blinds over the windows or wear an eye mask.
- An illuminated bedroom clock is a source of light that can be extremely annoying; try to avoid such clocks.
- Keep your bed for sleeping, not for watching TV or working.
- Go to bed at the same time and wake up in the morning at the same time, everyday.
- Do not take long nap in the daytime/afternoon as prolonged daytime naps steal hours from nighttime slumber.
- Instead of lying on the bed when you do not get sleep, do some reading or listen to soft music until you feel sleepy and tired.
- Some good bedtime habits are sleeping at the usual time, reading a book, listening to soothing music or taking a hot bath before going to bed.

- Get up at the same time every day, even on weekends and holidays.
- Once you have awakened, get up. Do not lie in bed awake, thinking about getting up.
- Do not lie in bed worrying about things. Find ways to reduce or manage the stress. Instead, do not entertain any thought that may make you feel tense.
- Do not drink any fluids within 2 hours of going to bed; this reduces the likelihood of needing to get up and go to the washroom in the mid of your sleep.
- Go to the bathroom right before bed, as this will reduce the chances that you will wake up in the middle of the night to attend nature's call.
- Remove the clock from view. It will only add to your worry when you constantly stare at it.
- Perform thirty minutes of Yoga/exercise everyday as this will tire the body, thus, inducing a refreshing sleep.
- Do exercise/Yoga regularly, especially the meditation or relaxation techniques.
- Do not exercise within 2 hours of bedtime as a workout soon before bedtime will interfere with your sleep.
- Have your dinner early and avoid eating a large meal within two hours of bedtime.

- Avoid caffeine, nicotine and alcohol at least 6 to 8 hours before bedtime as they all interfere with normal sleep.
- Avoid taking medicines that disrupt sleep.
- It is highly advisable to avoid sleeping pills without the consent of your doctor or physician.
- Avoid bright light around the house before bed.
- Avoid loud music, working on computers or stressful tasks before going to bed.
- Maintain a safe sleeping environment, free from harmful and sharp objects.
- If mosquitoes keep you awake, then use a mosquito repellant or coils to get rid of them.
- Insomnia is a problem related to sleep where the patient finds difficulty in falling or staying asleep.
- Some patients with insomnia may fall asleep easily but wake up soon while others may find trouble in sleeping easily and waking up late.
- Some insomniacs may have trouble with both, falling asleep and staying asleep.
- A poor-quality sleep is responsible for keeping the mind inactive throughout the day, and doesn't leave you feel refreshed when you wake up.
- Depression and illness are also closely associated with insomnia.
- An insomniac may suffer from poor concentration, impaired motor coordination and trouble in memorizing things.

- Narcolepsy is a chronic disorder related to the central nervous system that causes a person to have trouble staying awake.
- Narcolepsy can cause a person suddenly fall asleep during the daytime.
- People with narcolepsy can experience 'sleep attacks' even after getting enough sleep at night.
- The abnormal sleep pattern of people with narcolepsy can affect their schooling, work and social life.
- Sleep walking is a disorder that is characterized by complicated actions which result in walking during sleep.
- Sleepwalking can be harmless as well as dangerous to the individual.
- Snoring is a noise generated by vibration of the soft or floppy parts of the throat while breathing during sleep.
- People who snore may not be aware of their snoring.
- Snoring is more common in men as compared to women.
- Sometimes, snoring may lead to major sleep disorders such as upper respiratory resistance syndrome and obstructive sleep apnea. Do *anuloma-viloma pranayama* 5 to 10 minutes every day to get rid of snoring.

Our soul is a part of divine power but we are separated from him. We all should try to realize our true identity.

Who am I?

What is my goal of life?

What am I doing?

The life cycle in this world is "childhood-> student age->college->marriage->family->and finally we become aged and will be ready to say bye to this world". We all are so much busy in this cycle that we don't even think once that what our main purpose for coming in this life is. What is our aim for taking birth? Why we are so special than other creatures? To get all the answers I personally recommend attending the spiritual discourses in proper guidance of devotees (*Satsang*) and do self-study of holy scriptures. Spare sometime and develop a habit to read this timeless wisdom every day: *Upnishad, Gita, Srimad Bhagwatam* (*Bhakti* Yoga), Lord Buddha's teachings and other holy texts.

ABOUT 'WORLD WELFARE MISSION'

"Mission Health, Happiness, Peace and Welfare around the world"

- World Welfare Mission is a Volunteer based organisation, with a wide range of social, environmental, cultural and spiritual activities, reaches all walks of life.
- A non-profit, non-political, educational, humanitarian organization, it is committed to creating peace from the level of the individual upwards, and fostering human values within the global community.
- Pls. visit us at: http://www.worldwelfaremission.org The World Welfare Mission was set up in 2005 by Acharya Krishna Deo. A non-profit organization with a mission to work towards the betterment of the individual, the society and the world. World Welfare

Mission undertakes several social, environmental and holistic wellness programmes with the help of volunteers. World Welfare Mission is a non-political, non-religious organization based out of New Delhi and has a presence in several countries.

- Please avail the benefit of the programme as early as possible, to minimize/eliminate stress and ailments from individuals and society, as stress and ailments are increasing day by day because of our aberrant lifestyle......
- Email - worldwelfaremission@gmail.com

World Welfare Mission Highlights

1. **Mission Yoga**
   - To stop suicide cases worldwide, due to depression and ailments!
   - Strength and motivation to individuals & society towards positive life. Physical, Mental & Social!
   - Spreading 'YOGA' (The Holistic Traditional Art of India for more than 5000 years) to the world, for Health, Peace, Art of Happy Living and selfless service to individuals and society, to make this world more meaningful, strengthen, helpful and joyful...
2. **Mission Plantation**
   - We inspire people to plant, nurture and celebrate life!
   - To control global warming and pollution!

- Spreading awareness for our beautiful planet and encouraging people to plant more, stop destroying nature and protect environment.
- To make this planet a better place to live in...

3. Mission Education

- "*Vidya*" - The street education centers run by us.
- Educating and supporting unprivileged children for their overall development in rural and suburban area.
- Health care projects in remote area for unprivileged people. Free mobile health care (Health on wheel).

  To support our global mission for a cause please contact us at: worldwelfaremission@gmail.com

4. Social Welfare

- Pulse polio campaigning since 2006.
- Plantation since 2005.
- CSR (Corporate Social Responsibility) project partnership with organization, holistic wellness & Life Style Mgmt. programs.
- '*Vidya*' The street education points for underprivileged children.
- We welcome 'Mission Membership' donors to support the Mission.
- We welcome member of volunteers to support our service activities: Yoga *shivir, Satsang,* Plantation projects, Help Old age, financially weak students and people empowerment projects.

Future Vision

- '*Anandmay Jeevan Ashrams*' in different locations in India and abroad. That will work for Health, Happiness, Peace & Welfare around the world.

  Research institutes of Health, Healing & Happiness! *Gurukul* (Science & Spiritual Schools/Collages) to promote:

  Art of Blissful Life. Yoga & Nature Care. World Peace & *Seva* (Welfare)!

  For 'Mission Membership' please visit 'Donate' page of www.worldwelfaremission.org,

  or email us at: worldwelfaremission@gmail.com

Mission Membership

Mission Corporate Member Donation Rs. 11,00,000/- or (above)	Mission Honored Member Donation Rs. 51,000/- or (above)
Mission Founder Member Donation Rs. 5,51,000/- or (above)	Mission Respected Member Donation Rs. 21,000/- or (above)
Mission Parton Member Donation Rs. 2,51,000/- or (above)	Mission Life Member Donation Rs. 11,000/- or (above)
Mission Privileged Member Donation Rs. 1,00,000/- or (above)	Other........................

- Please visit our website

  www.worldwelfaremission.org

- Email- worldwelfaremission@gmail.com

You can forward/recommend this mission to likeminded people/organization for a good cause.

- Thank you so much for all your kind support for a great cause!

!! Om Shanti !!

Get associated: You can associate with World Welfare Mission in various ways.

1. **Corporate:**
   (i) Be part of a national level programme.
   (ii) Sponsor, wellness & welfare initiatives supported by World Welfare Mission.
   (iii) Invite World Welfare Mission to help establish projects under your CSR.
   (iv) Your employees can participate as volunteers for plantation and education projects.
   (v) Write to: worldwelfaremission@gmail.com

2. **Educational Institutions, Associations. Confederations, Development Organizations:**

   National and international organizations (educational institutions, donor organizations etc) can partner with World Welfare Mission under Alliances to further the development initiatives at grassroots level.

   Write to: worldwelfaremission@gmail.com

3. **Colleges, Students Associations:**

   Call/write for yoga and stress management classes/seminars. Or volunteer plantation and education projects

   email-worldwelfaremission@gmail.com

4. Individuals:

Volunteers: World Welfare Mission is looking for volunteers who can associate in different programmes and projects

To associate with

1. Yoga & Wellness *Shivir/Seminar*
2. Mission Education programme for underprivileged.
3. Mission Plantation Programme.
4. Healthcare on Wheels (Medical services on bus for remote areas).

   Write to worldwelfaremission@gmail.com

Support World Welfare Mission

- To promote Holistic Yoga & Art of Blissful Living seminars around the globe.
- To spread Health, Peace, Divine Love and selfless services.
- To make this world more peaceful and joyful.
- To plant more trees on earth. Support environment friendly projects.
- To educate and care more underprivileged children around the world.

Donations

Whether it is through cash contributions or donations in kind, time, or expertise, World Welfare Mission offers a variety of opportunities for you to extend your support.

Donations can be made directly to specific projects of your choice or to the general fund of the Mission that supports a host of activities.

Your contributions help us to reach out to more and more people offering opportunities and encouraging sustainable living, thus fulfilling our vision of creating a joyful, loving and peaceful world for all.

"Let us make it happen!"

"All this work involves an enormous amount of money and people with big hearts coming forth and working.

You can make your individual contribution in favour of "World Welfare Mission" by Cheque, DD, Online, NEFT/RTGS or by giving a letter of instruction to your bank, Monthly/Quarterly/Half yearly/Yearly/Life time mode of contribution, payable at Delhi, State Bank of India. A/c No-64105852543

IFSC/NEFT code:- SBIN0040478

(A)Rs.........(B)Rs.5100. (C)Rs.2100. (D)Rs.1100. (E) Rs. 500.

- One should donate 10% or at least 3% of his/her monthly income every month for a good cause.
- You can circulate Mission's massage to likeminded people through E-mail, your notice board etc.

Thanks a lot for all your genuine support...

Laughter yoga

Workshop for Indian Air Force

At hotel Hyatt

PROJECT ASHRAM

Anandmay Jeevan Ashram

The Project: A unique, International ***Ashram*** for spiritual seekers, who, they are looking for health, happiness, peace and divine love in life! Stay facilities for 2 days, 10 days or you can dedicate your life here. The person desirous of staying in this Ashram will first have to apply in writing by filling up a Registration form, with nationality Identity card, valid visa & passport. He/She has to be sponsored by another individual, group or organization. Age will not be a limited factor for applications because the whole concept revolves around the idea of spiritual seekers, and people looking for love, care, peace and spiritual upliftment. They will be allowed to stay here on a first come first serve basis for two days, seven days, nine days, one month, three months, or life time, depending on availability of space and need of the individual.

Funding: Several organizations and capable individuals from around the world have their intent to finance the project in cash or kind.

Working Capital: There will be two primary funding principals.

1. **Donation:** According to the tradition of pure *Vipassana*, courses are run solely on a donation basis. Donations are accepted only from those who have completed at least one course with Acharya Krishna Deo or one of his assisting teachers. Someone taking the course for the first time may give a donation on the last day of the course or any time thereafter.

   In this way courses are supported by those who have realized for themselves the benefits of the practice. Wishing to share these benefits with others, one gives a donation according to one's means and volition. Such donations are the only source of funding for course in this tradition around the world. There is no wealthy foundation or individual sponsoring them. Neither the teachers nor the organizers receive any kind of payment for their service. Thus, the spread of *Vipassana* is carried out with purity of purpose, free from any commercialism.

   Whether a donation is large or small, it should be given with the wish to help others: 'The course I have taken has been paid for through the generosity of past students; now let me give something towards the cost of a future course, so that others may also benefit by this technique.'

2. Mission Membership: People who will donate to the project as a one time or regular donor, under Mission Membership or without membership to

promote Health, Happiness, Peace & Social welfare around the world.

Silent Features: Peace Home for all.

This is a place where anyone (who have love and respect in their hearts for humanity) can stay. Separate rooms for ladies and gents, family and children.

Meditation Hall

Specially built for group Yoga/Meditation, Prayer and Spiritual discourses hall for all.

Living with Nature

There will be flower, fruit and herbal garden and provision for boating, musical fountains and waterfalls I Ashram premises to feel divine connectivity with nature.

Community Hall/Conference Hall

Eminent personalities/spiritual masters/Saints/scientists will be invited to give awareness, advices, and guidance, talks on Health, Happiness, Peace, Spirituality & Art of Happy living, personality development and soul upliftment.

Recreation Hall

To promote Music, Dance, Art, Humor, Play & ***Bhajan/Kirtan*** on spiritual and inspirational theme.

Rooms for stay: Rooms for residential workshops/meditation etc.

Annapurna: A Food Bank

There will be free ***satwik*** (***pure vegetarian***) food centre/common hall with kitchen where lunch and dinner will be served free of cost every day as ***Prasad*** (***desirous donor can donate separately for this Annapurna project***).

However, there will be a separate paid food centre also where herbal tea, snacks, breakfast, lunch and dinner can be purchased.

Book Stall: There will be a fully equipped book stall with health and spiritual books, life-inspiring books, and magazine for research and self-study.

Common Features: Administrative offices, Water Reservoir, Generator Room, Solar System etc.

Proposed feature in the future

- *Gurukul:* Residential school & Colleges.
- Research on *different paths of Yoga, Vedanta,* Holy Scriptures, *Naturopathy* and Art of Happy Living.
- Naturopathy Hospitals.
- **Herbal Plants Research & Production.**

Books of World Welfare Mission

1. Sahaj Krishna Yog- Pranayama & Mudra.
2. Shaj Krishna Yog- For Obesity.
3. Sahaj Krishna Yog- For Diabetes.
4. Sahaj Krishna Yog- For Hypertension
5. Sahaj Krishna Yog - For Stress Management.

6. Sahaj Krishna Yog- For Insomnia.
7. Sahaj Krishna Yog- For Women.
8. Sahaj Krishna Yog- For pregnant women/Prenatal Yoga.
9. Sahaj Krishna Yog- For Age 5-14 Years.
10. Sahaj Krishna Yog- Meditation.
11. Sahaj Krishna Yog –For Aged 60+
12. Sahaj Krishna Yog- To increase height.
13. Sahaj Krishna Yog- For Asthma.
14. Sahaj Krishna Yog- For Cervical and Back Pain.

!! Om Shanti !!

Workshop for college students

Corporate workshop

Corporate laughter yoga workshop

Workshop at Maharishi Ayurveda Hospital

With Yoga Participants from different countries

Corporate Stress Management Workshop L & T

Self-empowering Meditation
in the cave of Himalaya